THE UPPER ROOM

WHERE THE WORLD MEETS TO PRAY

Daniele Och
UK editor

INVITATIONAL
INTERDENOMINATIONAL
INTERNATIONAL

32 LANGUAGES
Multiple formats are available in some languages

BRF Ministries

15 The Chambers, Vineyard
Abingdon OX14 3FE
+44 (0)1865 319700 | brf.org.uk

Bible Reading Fellowship (BRF) is a charity (233280)
and company limited by guarantee (301324),
registered in England and Wales

EU Authorised Representative: Easy Access System Europe – Mustamäe tee 50, 10621
Tallinn, Estonia, **gpsr.requests@easproject.com**

ISBN 978 1 80039 392 9
All rights reserved

Originally published in the USA by The Upper Room® **upperroom.org**
US edition © 2025 The Upper Room, Nashville, TN (USA). All rights reserved.
This edition © Bible Reading Fellowship 2025
Cover photo by Anete Lusina/pexels.com

Acknowledgements

Scripture quotations marked with the following abbreviations are taken from the
version shown. Where no abbreviation is given, the quotation is taken from the same
version as the headline reference.

NIV: The Holy Bible, New International Version (Anglicised edition) copyright © 1979,
1984, 2011 by Biblica. Used by permission of Hodder & Stoughton Publishers, an
Hachette UK company. All rights reserved. 'NIV' is a registered trademark of Biblica.
UK trademark number 1448790.

NRSV: The New Revised Standard Version Updated Edition. Copyright © 2021
National Council of Churches of Christ in the United States of America. Used by
permission. All rights reserved worldwide.

CEB: copyright © 2011 by Common English Bible.

KJV: the Authorised Version of the Bible (The King James Bible), the rights in which
are vested in the Crown, are reproduced by permission of the Crown's Patentee,
Cambridge University Press.

A catalogue record for this book is available from the British Library

Printed and bound in the UK by Zenith Media NP4 0DQ

How to use *The Upper Room*

The Upper Room is ideal in helping us spend a quiet time with God each day. Each daily entry is based on a passage of scripture and is followed by a meditation and prayer. Each person who contributes a meditation seeks to relate their experience of God in a way that will help those who use *The Upper Room* every day.

Here are some guidelines to help you make best use of *The Upper Room*:

1 Read the passage of scripture. It is a good idea to read it more than once, in order to have a fuller understanding of what it is about and what you can learn from it.
2 Read the meditation. How does it relate to your own experience? Can you identify with what the writer has outlined from their own experience or understanding?
3 Pray the written prayer. Think about how you can use it to relate to people you know or situations that need your prayers today.
4 Think about the contributor who has written the meditation. Some users of *The Upper Room* include this person in their prayers for the day.
5 Meditate on the 'Thought for the day' and the 'Prayer focus', perhaps using them again as the focus for prayer or direction for action.

Why is it important to have a daily quiet time? Many people will agree that it is the best way of keeping in touch every day with the God who sustains us and who sends us out to do his will and show his love to the people we encounter each day. Meeting with God in this way reassures us of his presence with us, helps us to discern his will for us and makes us part of his worldwide family of Christian people through our prayers.

I hope that you will be encouraged as you use *The Upper Room* regularly as part of your daily devotions, and that God will richly bless you as you read his word and seek to learn more about him.

Helping to pay it forward

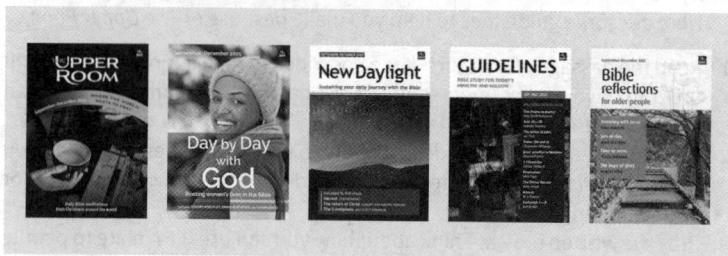

As part of our Living Faith ministry, we're raising funds to give away copies of Bible reading notes and other resources to those who aren't able to access them any other way, working with food banks and chaplaincy services, in prisons, hospitals and care homes. If you've enjoyed and benefited from our resources, would you consider paying it forward to enable others to do so too?

Make a gift at **brf.org.uk/donate**

thank
YOU
for all your support

A creative endeavour

Glory to God, who is able to do far beyond all that we could ask or imagine by his power at work within us.
Ephesians 3:20 (CEB)

When my grandmother taught me to knit when I was ten years old, I cast on stitches, envisioning a long, fluffy scarf to wrap around me in winter. Soon I saw I was creating a lopsided polygon that bore no resemblance to a scarf. The vision I had for my project did not match reality. Discouraged, I gave up.

Nearly a decade later, I tried knitting again, and came to it with a little more patience and coordination, and a willingness to reshape my vision as the project progressed. I corrected stitches, ripped out rows, and, eventually, I completed a scarf. I've since finished more knitting projects than I can count; and though I am much more skilled now, my finished projects almost never exactly match my initial vision. And that is part of the joy of creative projects – seeing where the journey leads.

Knitting has helped me think of the journey of faith as a creative endeavour. My idea of the best way to serve God doesn't always match up with the reality of what I can do or what the world truly needs. But God's vision for our service is much more expansive and imaginative than ours. In this issue of *The Upper Room*, writers share stories of unfulfilled dreams, life-altering illnesses and impossible mission projects that – with God's help – they reshaped into new, creative and life-giving ways of serving others and the world.

Scripture overflows with stories of God's creativity. Moses was rescued by the daughter of the Pharaoh who had ordered his execution (see Exodus 2:1–10); the wall surrounding Jericho fell when the Israelites marched around it sounding their trumpets (see Joshua 6:1–20); Jesus turned water into wine at a wedding in Cana (see John 2:1–11); and Christ overcame death on the cross, offering us eternal life. Imagine how we can change the world when we open ourselves to God's creative Spirit.

Lindsay Gray
Editorial director

English edition

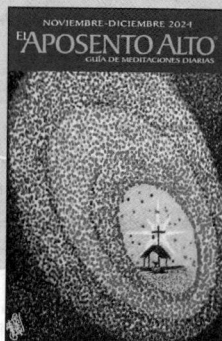

Spanish edition

Writers featured in this issue of *The Upper Room*:

Caribbean Netherlands: Arlene Timber-Henry
Dominican Republic: Julianis Báez de Pichardo,
Farlin Vanessa De Los Santos Mejía
Jamaica: Danelle Pinnock
Puerto Rico: Ángel Mattos de Jesús

Gifts to the international editions of
The Upper Room help the world meet to pray.
upperroom.org/gift

The editor writes...

The earth is the Lord's, and everything in it, the world, and all who live in it.
Psalm 24:1 (NIV)

One of the features of each day's meditation in *The Upper Room* is the prayer focus. As outlined on page 3, this, along with the 'thought for the day', is provided as an aid for prayer in response to the meditation for that day. Often the focus is something that, for me at least, sits comfortably within a time of prayer. In a prayer meeting, I would not be surprised for people to ask to pray for, for example, trust in God's strength, wisdom in daily decisions or a child they know who is undergoing surgery (see 5 September, 27 September and 25 November).

But I confess that sometimes I have wondered whether the prayer focus is, frankly, just too mundane. How do I pray for welders? What do jewellers need prayer about? And what about walkers and joggers – that's not even an occupation? (See 15 September, 20 October and 3 November.)

This is where I need a more thoroughly biblical view of creation and redemption. I need to recognise that when the psalmist says, 'The earth is the Lord's, and everything in it', that really does mean *everything*. Equally, God's desire to redeem creation extends to every aspect of it – 'to bring unity to all things in heaven and on earth under Christ' (Ephesians 2:10).

There are no aspects of life, therefore, that are too mundane to bring before God in prayer. As I pray for God's kingdom to come on earth as in heaven, I can think not only of how that applies to my personal spiritual growth or to the work of mission organisations and charities (such as BRF Ministries), but also of what that means for the work of welders, of jewellers and of the other occupations mentioned in this issue – indeed, even what it means for people doing something as mundane as going for a walk.

Daniele Och
UK editor

Spiritual treasures

Read Matthew 6:19–24

Store up for yourselves treasures in heaven, where neither moth nor rust consumes and where thieves do not break in and steal.
Matthew 6:20 (NRSV)

My husband and I are downsizing. Moving to a smaller home requires donating and discarding items in our current house. For me, this involves parting with an antique collection I acquired in the 90s with my brother Bob on our 'treasure hunts'. We were on quests to find relics from the past. Bob scoured shelves for childhood toys while I rummaged through boxes searching for antique tins with graphics from bygone eras.

Bob passed away many years ago, and the antiques displayed in my house remind me of those long-ago treasure hunts. But now it's time to part with them. In that earlier season of my life, collecting these treasures was a priority. Now as I put them all in a large box, today's scripture reading is on my mind.

Our earthly treasures, whether money, possessions or a collection of antiques, have no value in heaven. Instead, Jesus exhorts us to store up heavenly treasures. Worship and obedience to God, seeking God in scripture, supporting the church with my tithes, talents, and time, praying for the needs of others, being kind and encouraging, and sharing my faith through my writing are my spiritual treasures. They have value not only here but in my eternal home in heaven.

Prayer: *Lord Jesus, may our desire be to store up heavenly treasures, knowing that where our treasure is there our hearts will be also. Amen.*

Thought for the day: Spiritual treasures have eternal value.

Debra Pierce (Massachusetts, USA)

Divine wisdom

Read Proverbs 3:1–12

In their hearts humans plan their course, but the Lord establishes their steps.
Proverbs 16:9 (NIV)

Our church community was trying to decide on a project to address the increasing environmental pollution in our area. I placed the issue before the Lord in my daily prayers until one day, I felt the Lord asking me: 'Why not consider the welfare of those who are already taking care of my creation?' With the Lord's guidance, we all agreed to conduct a medical fair for the garbage collectors of the city, a forgotten community that renders an invaluable service to our society.

One of the biggest challenges we faced was finding the necessary funds. We approached prospective donors and asked volunteers for support. With the Lord's help, donations flowed in, and doctors and opticians volunteered their time. The city council authorities extended their full cooperation. Mobile medical testing vehicles were available to conduct health screenings. We were even able to provide attendees with a meal and with safety gear to use while working.

This project enabled us to share the love of God and to care for those who labour to keep God's creation clean. Tasks that are too big for us to accomplish on our own become possible through the grace and guidance of the Lord Jesus Christ.

Prayer: *Dear Lord, we praise and thank you for giving us the guidance and wisdom to execute our plans. Thank you for opportunities to bear witness to your love and care. Amen.*

Thought for the day: When I need guidance, I will place my concerns before God.

Nihal Cooray (Sri Lanka)

PRAYER FOCUS: GARBAGE COLLECTORS

Stronger together

Read Romans 15:1–6

*Live in harmony with one another… so that together you may with
one voice glorify the God and Father of our Lord Jesus Christ.*
Romans 15:5–6 (NRSV)

There are two sawmills in my state that cut and form desert mesquite
trees for furniture. This distinctive wood has a vivid and striking spectrum
of colour, shapes and swirls, but the mesquite is so dense that saw blades
dull after a few cuts. Despite being difficult to work with, mesquite has
greater structural integrity than other hardwoods because of its tight
grain pattern, which makes the wood less likely to warp, crack or split.

Several years ago a Bible drive at our church brought similar 'structural
integrity' to the congregation. We collected Bibles and other Christian
literature to send overseas to believers hungry for the word of God. Con-
gregants of all ages became strongly motivated with this assignment,
scouring their homes for any extra Bibles and Christian resources. The
project brought people together.

Unity within the body of Christ is an important message in Paul's
letters. It's not just a matter of diverse people getting along but also
sharing goals to bring glory to God. Like the mesquite's dramatic beauty,
superior strength and tightly woven pattern, churches thrive when we
live in harmony, participating together in spreading the love of Christ.

Prayer: *Dear God, bless all who organise outreach ministries.
Thank you for all who work together to share the good news of your
love with others. Amen.*

Thought for the day: Our ministry grows stronger when we are
united in purpose.

Beverly Taylor (Arizona, USA)

Through it all

Read John 1:1–5

Through him all things were made; without him nothing was made that has been made.
John 1:3 (NIV)

When I was diagnosed with stage-four breast cancer at 27 years old, I became aware of God's constant presence in a whole new way. God was with me during my suffering as well as my healing process and eventual remission, which I still celebrate over 20 years later. God was working through the doctors, my friends and the other people who helped me during this major life crisis.

I used to think God was only present in the good, 'holy' moments I experienced. But I discovered that God is always with me, regardless of whether I perceive God's presence. I learned to reframe my thinking about who God is and God's nature. Instead of thinking of God as distant, merely watching me fail as a human, I began to see God as scripture describes – everywhere and in all things.

God is always with us, and nothing can change that fact. No matter what we do or what happens in our lives, God guides and loves us through it all.

Prayer: *Dear God, thank you for being with us in sorrow and in joy. Help us to notice your presence and to trust that you are at work in our lives. Amen.*

Thought for the day: God's love surrounds me today and every day.

Elizabeth M. (Washington, USA)

Source of strength

Read 2 Corinthians 4:1–15

We have this treasure in jars of clay to show that this all-surpassing power is from God and not from us.
2 Corinthians 4:7 (NIV)

Sometimes it seems like everything is going wrong all at once – as if the world is collapsing around us. When life is going awry, it can be easy to fall into despair. Personally, this tempts me to numb myself with over-eating or watching too much TV and to neglect my regular prayer time.

But scripture gives us another answer. It tells us that our weakness is made perfect by God's strength. The very fact that we can become distressed by the burdens of life shows that it is not our own strength that helps us endure. Christians do not have more willpower or grit than non-believers. Rather, it is the power of our mighty God that helps us to persist.

When we are pressed on every side, are perplexed or paralyzed by indecision, are persecuted for our faith or are rejected and struck down, we need not despair – God promises that we will not be crushed and will never be abandoned. We can persevere in God's strength and stand firm in the power of our loving Saviour.

Prayer: *All-powerful God, we give you the hardships of this day. We pray that when we feel beaten down by life, we will remember that you are mightier than our problems. Amen.*

Thought for the day: In life's struggles, I can lean on the strength of my creator and redeemer.

Jillian Bell (Ontario, Canada)

The gift of sight

Read Acts 9:1–17

Saul got up from the ground, and though his eyes were open, he could see nothing; so they led him by the hand and brought him into Damascus.

Acts 9:8 (NRSV)

After reading a devotion in *The Upper Room* about the gift of being an organ donor, I felt convicted to share my perspective as an organ recipient. In my late 20s, I was diagnosed with keratoconus, a degenerative corneal disease that can require corneal transplantation. With my vision uncorrected, I was legally blind.

When I was 42 years old, I was like Saul – a self-reliant, lukewarm believer. But one morning, I woke up blind in one eye. My ophthalmologist said I needed a corneal transplant. After two transplants, my vision is nearly perfect. I was amazed at the clarity I had been missing all those years. Most certainly, the praise and honour goes to God the Father, but I also honour the two donors, both of whom I think of as Ananias.

Every day I look in the mirror, thankful to the donors who gave me the gift of physical sight. As I pray each day, I thank God for these donors and for sending Jesus as my Lord and Saviour. Jesus and the donors have both offered generous love to me. These gifts inspire me to live a life committed to following Christ.

Prayer: *Sovereign God, we thank you for the grace and mercy you extend to us every day. In Jesus' name, we pray. Amen.*

Thought for the day: I am thankful for the generous love Christ shows to me.

Victor Carcioppolo (Ohio, USA)

Unexpected blessings

Read Ruth 2:1–16

I'm sure about this: the one who started a good work in you will stay with you to complete the job by the day of Christ Jesus.
Philippians 1:6 (CEB)

One summer morning I noticed a lily blooming in my garden. It was such a pleasant surprise! This species of lily generally blooms during the rainy season, not during the scorching summer. But there it was, standing tall, waving in the wind.

Even though I had been unaware of it, my lily's bloom had been developing for a long time. The plant's cells organised to form a bud, nutrients and water nourished the plant, and the lily gradually grew a blooming flower. God had prepared the plant in advance to produce a flower, but the preparation was unseen.

Just like my lilies, life often brings beautiful, unexpected surprises that rejuvenate our soul. These events don't happen out of the blue; they are all planned by the Lord.

Many times we wait hopefully on the Lord for our desires to be fulfilled. We may not even be aware of the preparation taking place in our lives. Who knows what is best for us better than the Lord? We might feel like our life is dull or unproductive, but as we wait upon the Lord, he prepares us for what is still to come. The next thing may unexpectedly bloom one day, just like my lily.

Prayer: *Caring God, we trust you with our needs and our desires. We lay our burdens at your feet, believing that you are preparing us for what lies ahead. Amen.*

Thought for the day: Even when I am waiting, I will keep trusting the Lord.

Deepika Emmanuel Sagar (Waikato, New Zealand)

A generous spirit

Read Luke 6:27–38

Give, and it will be given to you. A good measure, pressed down, shaken together and running over, will be poured into your lap. For with the measure you use, it will be measured to you.
Luke 6:38 (NIV)

Decades ago, I had a friend who needed financial assistance. I helped her because she needed it and I was able to. Years later, when my own finances were in shambles, an old college friend came to my rescue. At that time I had little money to spare and struggled to make it from one month to the next.

I remember getting a cheque in the mail a week before I was due to receive my disability income. I went to the bank to cash it. The rules of the bank required me to have enough money in my account to cover the face value of the cheque, and I did not. The bank supervisor must have sensed my desperation and made an exception to the rule and cashed it anyway. Relief washed over me. Not long after that, I made a donation to a Christian organisation, feeling very thankful for kind deeds and for God's angels who have helped me.

God encourages us to carry each other's burdens, to love one another. The good Samaritan recognised this. I have had the good fortune and blessing to be in both positions – blessed to be needed and humbled to need. And I've learned that generosity is not about the amount of money you have to give. It's about your willingness to be kind – to give and receive with an open heart.

Prayer: *God of bounty, nurture within us a spirit of generosity that is eager to help others as we have been helped. Amen.*

Thought for the day: It is a blessing both to give and to receive.

Janet R. Parker (Connecticut, USA)

Humble prayer

Read James 4:7–10

When you pray, go to your room, shut the door, and pray to your Father who is present in that secret place. Your Father who sees what you do in secret will reward you.
Matthew 6:6 (CEB)

Following eight months of unemployment I reluctantly accepted a position that separated me from my family by 1,440 miles. After nine months apart from my wife and children, the feeling of accomplishment at having a job turned to frustration. The separation from my family began to drain me. I felt isolated in the small town where my job was located, so I watched a lot of TV.

One evening, my emotions were at an all-time low. I could not envision any solution that would allow me to regain a normal family life. At that very moment the preacher I had been watching on TV spoke about humbling oneself in prayer before God. As he called for viewers to kneel before God and pray for solutions to their troubles, I knelt before the television set and asked God to guide me to a solution to my situation. I confessed that I could not find an answer alone; I needed God's help.

Three months later a new position became available back in the town where my family was located, and I was selected to fill it. We were reunited. Although a variety of situations may confront us during our lifetime, I have learned that the single best solution to resolve them is humble prayer.

Prayer: *Listening God, thank you for hearing our personal problems. We cannot solve them alone and humbly look to you for guidance. Amen.*

Thought for the day: Earnest prayer is the best solution to my problems.

John Alter (Florida, USA)

A surprise opportunity

Read Galatians 3:23–29

You are a chosen people, a royal priesthood, a holy nation, God's special possession, that you may declare the praises of him who called you out of darkness into his wonderful light.
1 Peter 2:9 (NIV)

The printer got ahead of itself and started to print multiple pages at once – then it jammed. I took it to the technician I usually worked with, and he told me he would have to take it apart.

I went back the following day, hoping the printer was fixed because I needed to print the liturgy for Sunday's worship service. The technician explained that he had cleared the jam and gotten the printer running again. I was about to pay him when he said: 'No need. When one receives a blessing, one should give a blessing. I read some of what you wrote as I extracted pages from the printer. I came to know about God as an adult, which was a great blessing for me; it changed my life. As I read some of your writings, I felt God was continuing to bless me.'

I was moved by this surprise from God. The technician and I had never spoken about our faith. But this encounter gave us the opportunity to speak about God and faith, give thanks for the presence of God, and recognise each other as kindred spirits. We had the assurance of knowing we are children of God.

Prayer: *Thank you, Lord, for opportunities to meet other people of faith and share in the joy of following Christ. Amen.*

Thought for the day: Every day God surprises me with blessings.

Cristina Dinoto (Mendoza, Argentina)

Never too old

Read Genesis 12:1–8

Is not wisdom found among the aged? Does not long life bring understanding?
Job 12:12 (NIV)

It was a sad moment for me when I retired from full-time ministry almost ten years ago. I missed leading worship, the people and other aspects of my role as church leader – though I admit the administration and bureaucracy left me cold. To continue to worship within the same denomination, my wife and I travelled to another town. We kept this up for a few years, but eventually decided to worship in the town where we live and joined another church.

We received a wonderful welcome. I was eventually asked if I would lead worship at a small chapel, and couldn't refuse. As time passed, the minister indicated he was intending to apply for an assistant. I immediately said, 'Look no further,' and the rest is history.

God can use us notwithstanding our age; we are never too old to answer God's call. Abraham was 75 when he was called by God to leave his country, his people, and his father's household to travel the vast distance to Canaan. And as Job testifies, those in later life can have much wisdom to offer. By responding to God's call, an exciting journey is laid before us.

Prayer: *Heavenly Father, thank you for the joy and privilege of serving you at all stages of our lives. Amen.*

Thought for the day: 'The righteous… will still bear fruit in old age' (Psalm 92:12–14).

John Hauselman (England, United Kingdom)

The right time

Read Ecclesiastes 3:1–8

*Do not be anxious about anything, but in everything by prayer
and supplication with thanksgiving let your requests be made known
to God.*
Philippians 4:6 (NRSV)

The start of spring was very exciting for me because my yard was growing grass in places that had been bare for years. Because the grass was new, the man who maintains my yard told me I would need to wait longer to cut it. He explained that the new grass needed ample time to take root. My neighbour, who is a lawn expert, agreed. So for two weeks I watched my grass flourish; but soon it started to look more like a jungle! Every time I asked for it to be cut, I got the same reply – it's not time.

I began to get impatient because my yard looked like a wild forest compared to the yards of my neighbours. Then God reminded me once again to be patient and trust the process. What looked wild to me was in the perfect condition for God to transform it into something beautiful – all in the right time.

Today I encourage us all to wait on God's timing in the situations we face. What looks like chaos to us could be the perfect scenario for God to be God. God is aware of every challenging situation we encounter and already has a plan for resolving it. So let's pray, be patient and let God bring transformation.

Prayer: *Dear Father, help us to remain patient in every season and to focus on your guiding presence. Amen.*

Thought for the day: Be still and let God be God.

Mitzi Fears (Georgia, USA)

The wonder of creation

Read Psalm 104:10–26

Lord, you have done so many things! You made them all so wisely! The earth is full of your creations!
Psalm 104:24 (CEB)

Our dog Madani has recently given birth to three cuddly puppies. It seems like every move the puppies make is cuteness overload. I have watched them grow quickly from having their eyes closed to learning how to crawl to learning to walk.

As I reflect on our little puppies, I'm reminded of the psalmist praising God for the vastness of creation. Psalm 104 details how God has intricately designed each precious creation. Nature proclaims the greatness of our creator. All creation gives God glory.

Looking at our puppies, I can't help but love them and enjoy them. Likewise, I believe God enjoys the magnificence of creation, loving, caring for and providing for us all.

Prayer: *Lord God Almighty, we thank you for your beautiful creation and for the ways it reminds us of your great love. We pray as Jesus taught us, 'Our Father which art in heaven, Hallowed be thy name. Thy kingdom come, Thy will be done in earth, as it is in heaven. Give us this day our daily bread. And forgive us our debts, as we forgive our debtors. And lead us not into temptation, but deliver us from evil: For thine is the kingdom, and the power, and the glory, for ever. Amen'*
(Matthew 6:9–13, KJV).

Thought for the day: God speaks to me through creation.

Karen M. (Manila, Philippines)

You matter

Read 1 Thessalonians 5:12–18

We urge you, brothers and sisters, warn those who are idle and disruptive, encourage the disheartened, help the weak, be patient with everyone.
1 Thessalonians 5:14 (NIV)

I have been involved in prison ministry since 2016. Once I received an email from a woman in federal prison that said, 'The Christmas celebration with you guys was incredible. It made me feel like I mattered.' I was stunned by the second sentence. I thought, *Of course you matter! To me and especially to God.* That was obvious to me but apparently not always to her. I realised that too often the world tells and shows these women that they do not matter.

Many who are incarcerated feel rejected and abandoned. Understanding this made me realise the importance of letting people know that they matter to God and to me. We can help people to know God's love through our words and actions. On more than one occasion, women at the jail have told me that they cried when they read the words 'You matter' in a note I have sent to them. We may not always know the effect our words have on someone, but an encouraging word and our support can mean a great deal to others.

Prayer: *Dear Lord, help us to reach out to others with words and acts of kindness, encouragement, support and love, so that they will know how much they matter to you. Amen.*

Thought for the day: I can encourage others with my words and actions.

Julie Breutzmann (Iowa, USA)

Not alone

Read John 16:1–7

'The Advocate, the Holy Spirit, whom the Father will send in my name, will teach you all things and will remind you of everything I have said to you.'
John 14:26 (NIV)

My father was my first welding instructor. He taught me the basics, which became the foundation for my continued improvement. Then I went to welding school and worked with more experienced welders to learn my trade. Over the years, I gained skill and experience as I worked on more advanced welding projects. However, even as I improved, there were times when I would get stuck on a welding problem. I could always call my father, and he would give me advice on how to solve it.

Then my father passed away, and a couple of weeks after the funeral, I got stuck on another welding problem. As usual, I thought, *I'll call my father*. I was halfway to the telephone before I realised that I couldn't do that anymore. I suddenly felt very alone. I went back to the project, realising I was now on my own and had to use my own skills to solve the problem.

I think this is how the disciples must have felt when Jesus said he had to leave them. John's gospel says they were 'filled with grief'. They felt they would never again have a relationship with him or learn from him. However, Jesus promised to send the Holy Spirit to be in relationship with us and guide us. We are not alone. We have the Spirit guiding us always.

Prayer: *Dear Father, thank you for sending the Holy Spirit to comfort us and guide us on life's journey. Amen.*

Thought for the day: With the Spirit as my guide, I can go forward in confidence.

David Coxton (Michigan, USA)

The right path

Read Psalm 23

He guides me along the right paths for his name's sake. Even though I walk through the darkest valley, I will fear no evil, for you are with me; your rod and your staff, they comfort me.
Psalm 23:3–4 (NIV)

I was depressed, weighed down by decisions I made that were clearly not aligned with the values of a Christ-filled life and were leading me down the wrong path. One morning I opened my Bible looking for answers and seeking to return to Christ and his teachings. The Spirit of the Lord led me to Psalm 23.

Later that day, I was involved in a serious car accident. God's divine presence was surely with me that day, and the scripture I had read earlier in the day provided me with strength and comfort for what was to come. More than that, it allowed me to fully acknowledge that even though I had abandoned God, God had never abandoned me. God has been with me through the darkest valleys and guides me still. Thanks be to God!

Prayer: *Faithful God, we know that when we pull away from you, you never abandon us. Thank you for your patience and for your steadfast love and forgiveness. Amen.*

Thought for the day: God will never abandon me.

Sindy Magaly Cuchala Morales (Colombia)

Dave's wave

Read 1 Peter 4:8–11

Each of you should use whatever gift you have received to serve others, as faithful stewards of God's grace in its various forms.
1 Peter 4:10 (NIV)

My friend Dave suffers from severe Parkinson's disease. He now needs a wheelchair, speaks in a whisper and cannot lift his head. Although Dave has limitations, every weekday he gives what he has to hundreds of people in his community.

In the afternoon before school lets out, Dave wheels his chair down to the end of the driveway and waves to the buses filled with school children. When he feels strong enough, Dave tips his cap to the boys and girls who look forward to seeing their 'driveway friend'. On most days the bus drivers slow down so the children can cheer and call out greetings like 'I love you, Dave.' Dave was once a healthy man and an athlete. Even though he is now dependent on the people who once depended on him, Dave hasn't stopped giving to others.

God doesn't ask us to give what we don't have, but God does expect us to give what we do have. Even when we feel cast aside by declining health, limited finances, family estrangement or other adversities, we still have gifts and talents God can use to minister to others. Remembering Dave's wave, we can ask God to show us how to use what we have been given to bless others.

Prayer: *Dear God, help us to appreciate all that you have given us and to use our lives to bless others. Amen.*

Thought for the day: I will not let personal adversities keep me from loving others.

Elizabeth Erlandson (Nebraska, USA)

Rescuing hands

Read Luke 10:25–37

'A Samaritan, as he travelled, came where the man was; and when he saw him, he took pity on him. He went to him and bandaged his wounds, pouring on oil and wine. Then he put the man on his own donkey, brought him to an inn and took care of him.'
Luke 10:33–34 (NIV)

One evening while checking on our cattle, my dad and I found an orphaned newborn calf with one of her hooves stuck in barbed wire. She was exhausted and unable to stand. We carried her through the pasture to our car, then drove her home, worried she wouldn't survive the night.

Our family bottle-fed the calf for over a month until she could eat grain. She grew quickly and regained the ability to walk. Now she has raised calves of her own. She still remembers my father and walks up to him to lick his shoes.

Often when all hope seems lost, God reaches out to us through others to offer a rescuing hand. Recall how the good Samaritan assisted the man who was beaten half to death: first bandaging the man's wounds, then placing him on his donkey and taking him to an inn to receive care.

Opportunities to spread the love of God to others abound. God may direct us to help others when they are struggling with illness, addiction, grief, financial hardships or other difficult situations. Opportunities to receive help are also all around us. We never know how a life may be uplifted when we offer help.

Prayer: *Merciful God, help us to reach out to others when we witness them struggling. And may we not hesitate to reach out when we need a helping hand. Amen.*

Thought for the day: Helping others is easy when I use the gifts God has provided.

Daniel Bollinger (Missouri, USA)

Partners in ministry

Read Exodus 4:10–17

'He will speak to the people for you, and it will be as if he were your mouth and as if you were God to him.'
Exodus 4:16 (NIV)

'Can you take care of the children on Tuesday night?' asked a friend in my church. I was going to say no because I had no experience in children's ministry, but then I thought, *Why don't I try? After all, this would be an opportunity to serve God.* Before I agreed, I asked her if I would have a partner, and she said that I would. Praise God, the evening went well. The children enjoyed their time with my partner and me.

Later, I thought of Moses. Like me, he was not at all confident when God commanded him to bring the Israelites out of Egypt. He had no experience as a leader. But God understood Moses' hesitation and provided a partner for him – his brother Aaron. With Aaron by his side, Moses fulfilled his command from God successfully. Finally, the Israelites escaped Egypt under Moses' inspired leadership.

We cannot always do God's work alone, but we don't have to. Sometimes God gives us a partner. Scripture shows many examples: Eve for Adam (see Genesis 2—3); Deborah for Barak (see Judges 4); Silas for Paul (see Acts 15:40). God will bring us people who care for us and who will share our ministry with us.

Prayer: *Dear God, thank you for never leaving us to fend for ourselves. We thank you for people who care for us and help us in the work you have given us to do. Amen.*

Thought for the day: God provides what I need to obey the call to serve.

Linawati Santoso (East Java, Indonesia)

Needing the light

Read Matthew 5:14–16

'Let your light shine before others, so that they may see your good works and give glory to your Father in heaven.'
Matthew 5:16 (NRSV)

My infertility journey was an incredibly long and lonely time. Friends and co-workers were all having babies seemingly on demand. Even those that needed medical assistance were able to conceive, but I wasn't. My mum cared, but she had three children so I never felt like she could relate to my pain. I tried a Christian support group, but the leader had four children. There was no way she understood my struggles. I looked to books, including the Bible, but all were full of stories of women who struggled with infertility, held on to faith and eventually had children. I longed for a light to let me know I wasn't alone.

A complete hysterectomy in my early 40s forced me to realise I would never have a baby. I felt like a failure and was grieving. Then one week my adult Sunday school class had a lesson mentioning that God sent us to be the light. This made a big impression on me. I was already volunteering in the community, but this reminded me that others struggle with their own darkness. I tried remembering all the blessings I did have. I looked for ways to shine light for others. On tough days I still grieve and wonder why I wasn't given children, but I count my blessings and look for someone who can benefit from a little light from me.

Prayer: *Loving God, give us strength to handle loss and to look for others needing your light. Amen.*

Thought for the day: God will show me someone who needs my light today.

Jill Collins Spencer (North Carolina, USA)

The words of a child

Read Mark 10:13–16

He said to them, 'Let the little children come to me, and do not hinder them, for the kingdom of God belongs to such as these.'
Mark 10:14 (NIV)

It was Saturday, and I still had not selected a sermon topic. I prayed for help or some sign, but I was just nervous and preoccupied. I was still trying to organise my thoughts when my eight-year-old son, Manuel, approached me. The night before, I had been a bit harsh with him because of some mischief he had gotten into, so I stopped working on my sermon topic briefly to ask him for forgiveness. I continued talking to him for a few minutes about the forgiveness God offers us.

While talking to Manuel I mentioned that I was trying to write my sermon but was not having much success, as he could see from my blank computer screen. Then I asked that he run along so I could get back to work. Manuel fixed his eyes on me and asked, 'Why don't you write about what you just told me?' He then took off.

God had answered my prayer! I had my sermon material and the title: 'God forgives'. This experience with my young son helped me become even more aware of the importance of children within the kingdom of God and the ways God can speak to us through children.

Prayer: *Gracious Lord, help us be a guiding light for others – especially children. Help us to listen attentively to them and to you. Amen.*

Thought for the day: God speaks to me through all God's children, so I will listen.

Ángel Mattos de Jesús (Puerto Rico)

Encourage one another

Read 1 Corinthians 1:1–9

Continue encouraging each other and building each other up,
just like you are doing already.
1 Thessalonians 5:11 (CEB)

In July 2006 I lost my 25-year-old son, Daniel, to ALS – also known as Lou Gehrig's disease. It was a dark time in my life. I knew God was there, but I questioned everything.

My son was a kind, encouraging and loving person with a very generous heart. Daniel never lost his loving and caring nature. Even when the doctors told him there was no cure, he looked at me and said, 'Mum, don't you worry; God's got a plan.' Even as he faced the future knowing he would never be well again, he gave me encouragement. Daniel reminded me to trust God no matter what. He helped me to remember how important it is to love and encourage one another.

God gave my son a heart to encourage others. 'Encourage one another' may sound trite, but it can make all the difference in someone's life. So let's not hesitate to share an encouraging word. We never know whom we might help.

Prayer: *Dear Lord, teach us to encourage one another so that we may bless others and also be blessed. Amen.*

Thought for the day: Today I will encourage someone.

Betty L. Martin (North Carolina, USA)

Superior wisdom

Read Proverbs 2:1–11

Wisdom will enter your mind, and knowledge will fill you with delight. Discretion will guard you; understanding will protect you.
Proverbs 2:10–11 (CEB)

The fuel gauge in my car was erratic. The needle was all over the place. Sometimes it showed 'Empty' when I knew I had not driven more than 25 miles since filling the tank. There were no leaks; the gauge was simply giving an incorrect reading. Knowing the gauge must be wrong but being so accustomed to relying on it, I became confused and concerned. An instrument I had once depended on could no longer be trusted. Eventually, I took the car to a mechanic who diagnosed and fixed the problem.

This experience reminded me that while worldly measures or indicators can give us false or inaccurate readings, God's word never does. When we are confused or find some 'wisdom' of the world to be untrustworthy, we can go to God's word to find help; we can rely on God's superior wisdom by praying for God's guidance.

Just as I eventually took my car to a trusted mechanic for help with this issue, it is important that we ask our omniscient God for discernment and direction and remain alert for God's answer in whatever form it may come.

Prayer: *Loving, all-knowing God, help us always to seek your wisdom first and foremost. Amen.*

Thought for the day: God's wisdom can be trusted.

April Bogert (New York, USA)

God with us

Read Exodus 33:12–23

The Lord said to Moses, 'I will do the very thing you have asked, because I am pleased with you and I know you by name.'
Exodus 33:17 (NIV)

I'm almost 30 years old, but I have never travelled alone – until now. I feel like I've been cooped up in my comfort zone. And as safe as that feels, I recognise that it hinders my growth. I'm at a point in my life where I want to challenge myself.

With my bags packed, I went to Mass before heading off on my trip. As I entered the church, I knew what my prayers would be – to ask for God's guidance and to lay down my fears. During the priest's message, he reminded us of the name *Immanuel*, emphasising its meaning: God with us (see Matthew 1:18–25). This reminder was all I needed to calm my doubts and fears about my trip. I had not yet voiced my prayers, but God had answered me already through the priest's message. God knows our prayers, as well as our doubts and fears, before we utter them.

In today's scripture reading, Moses talks with God and asks for guidance and favour as he and the Israelites travel to the promised land. God assures Moses that God will be with them, even though they will not be able to see God. By faith we know that God is with us and always will be.

Prayer: *Dear God, thank you for being with us always. May our thoughts, words and deeds glorify you. Amen.*

Thought for the day: God knows me and calls me by name.

Jether Ann F. Rizaldo (Benguet, Philippines)

A gift of laughter

Read 1 Corinthians 10:10–13

God shall supply all your need according to his riches in glory by Christ Jesus.
Philippians 4:19 (KJV)

It was an awful day at work. I was tired and stressed from having to work at a fast pace. My earplugs were uncomfortable, and the loud, rumbling machines only made my headache worse. Our assembly line was nearly ten parts behind with more parts coming down the line. I considered just giving up on the day and catching a ride home.

Instead, during my first break of the day I prayed, 'God, I've made it this far. Please help me make it through the rest of my shift.' Returning to the line after break, the situation hadn't improved. We were working to catch up, but it didn't matter. When it was time for my second break, I felt ready to explode! This time I prayed, 'God, I've had all I can take. Please help me and the others. If you don't do something, Lord, I'm going to lose it!'

I trudged back to the line where my co-workers were still scrambling to catch up but to no avail. But instead of being consumed again by frustration, I started laughing! There was no good reason to laugh, but laughter flowed out of me like a rushing stream. And the peace I felt was liberating!

When my shift was over, ten parts were left on the floor for third shift, and the boss was not pleased. But my earlier frustration was gone. The gift of laughter God had given me was just what I needed to carry me through when I felt I couldn't go on.

Prayer: *Dear heavenly Father, thank you for the gift of laughter that makes life so much more bearable and enjoyable. In Jesus' name we pray. Amen.*

Thought for the day: God's gift of laughter lightens my load.

Tyler Myers (Ohio, USA)

Using my grief

Read 1 Peter 1:3–7
He heals the broken-hearted and binds up their wounds.
Psalm 147:3 (NIV)

When I was only two, my 15-year-old sister died by suicide. As I grew up, the shadow of grief was all-encompassing. It was strange to be grieving someone I could barely remember.

For most of my early teenage years, I was in a constant simmer of anger – at the world and at God. It wasn't until I returned to church and started grief counselling that my relationship with God began to heal. Through my counsellor, God helped me process my grief so that I could continue to live my life fruitfully despite the pain I faced at such a young age.

When I was a senior in high school, I felt for the first time that I was called to go to university. The path God had planned for me was finally visible. I felt the need to get my degree in psychology, to be a therapist for teenagers and young adults. I wanted to help those who are struggling in the way my sister did. I believe that despite the trauma I've been facing most of my life, God has a plan to use my grief experiences to help those who are facing similar pain.

If you or someone you know is in crisis or experiencing suicidal thoughts, call the Samaritans on 116 123.

Prayer: *Dear God, may the plans you have for us prosper as you heal our wounds. Amen.*

Thought for the day: The pain I experience equips me to show God's love to others.

Brianna Sligar (Texas, USA)

Desiring wisdom

Read Proverbs 8:1–11

Wisdom is more precious than rubies, and nothing you desire can compare with her.
Proverbs 8:11 (NIV)

What do you desire? Does wisdom top your list? If I were honest with God and myself, I would have to admit that although wisdom is on my list, it isn't the first thing. My immediate wishes are more along the lines of peaceful relationships, not to be cut off in rush hour, or a waterproof phone since my last one broke after getting wet at the pool. While there is nothing wrong with desiring those things, Proverbs 8:11 challenges my choices and makes me wonder: *why is wisdom so much more desirable than anything else?*

As we read the book of Proverbs, we learn quite quickly why wisdom is supreme: it knows that the path to life is found by keeping God at the centre of all we do and following God's commands. By doing this, we can stay on the path that is blessed by God and find peace in our relationships, patience for the shortcomings of others and contentment with what God has given us. However, the greatest blessing is that this path leads to eternal life, and there is nothing more precious than that.

Prayer: *Merciful God, help us set our hearts on following the path of your wisdom. Guide us to experience the blessings you have for us. Amen.*

Thought for the day: I will follow God's path of wisdom.

Connie Siedler (Auvergne-Rhône-Alpes, France)

Like a child

Read Psalm 86:1–7

This is the confidence we have in approaching God: that if we ask anything according to his will, he hears us.
1 John 5:14 (NIV)

Nine-year-old Emmie raised her hand with a prayer concern during our church service. First, she requested prayer for the people experiencing war in Ukraine. And then she asked for prayer to be able to make a sound when she blew into her flute. Apparently, she had just begun to take flute lessons, and only silence had prevailed!

What a lovely example of prayer. With her first request, Emmie was thinking about others, asking for the working of God's peaceful presence in conflict. Her second request was personal – the longing of a young musician's heart. It was very important to Emmie but maybe not to anyone else. Yet God desires for us to bring all our concerns to God.

God cares for the whole world and for us personally with the same amount of love, mercy and compassion.

Prayer: *Dear Lord, may we confidently bring our concerns to you, trusting that you care about each one. Amen.*

Thought for the day: God cares for me and my concerns – big and small.

Lin Daniels (Massachusetts, USA)

God walks with us

Read Philippians 4:4–9

The Lord is close to everyone who calls out to him,
to all who call out to him sincerely.
Psalm 145:18 (CEB)

As I get older, it seems I am needing to have more medical procedures. Frequency, however, does not diminish my anxiety about the procedures. What does help is remembering to pray first – and not just silent, under-my-breath prayers. Right before a procedure gets started, I ask the doctor or dentist if they mind if I say a short prayer. I then ask God to bless those in the room, to guide the doctor's hands and to bring me good results with speedy healing.

So far, no one has objected. As a matter of fact, occasionally I will see the doctor's face become calmer as we all take a minute to stop and talk to God – a short respite in their otherwise hectic day. These moments of prayer help me remember not to focus on what is about to happen to me but rather to focus on God walking through it with me.

Prayer: *Dear God, please help us remember to come to you with our needs, both large and small. We know that you are there for us whenever we need you. Walk with us, as we pray the prayer Jesus taught us: 'Our Father in heaven, hallowed be your name, your kingdom come, your will be done, on earth as it is in heaven. Give us today our daily bread. And forgive us our debts, as we also have forgiven our debtors. And lead us not into temptation, but deliver us from the evil one' (Matthew 6:9–13, NIV). Amen.*

Thought for the day: In anxious moments, I will take time to pray.

Kim Koratsky (Tennessee, USA)

Seasoned with salt

Read Acts 17:22–34

Let your conversation be always full of grace, seasoned with salt, so that you may know how to answer everyone.
Colossians 4:6 (NIV)

I made a chocolate cake and served it for teatime, but nobody looked happy. Then I tasted it, and it was bland. My husband took one bite and declared, 'You forgot the salt!' The recipe called for a quarter-teaspoon of salt, which I had omitted. Even in sweet dishes, a tiny amount of salt makes all the difference.

In a similar way, it is important to correctly season our conversations so that we can make a difference. Each conversation requires a unique approach. It is important to be gracious and encouraging as we share our thoughts and what we know with others. In Acts 17, Paul gives us a beautiful example to follow. Even though he was distressed to see all the idols in Athens, he complimented the Greek people on being very religious (see vv. 16–22). They had numerous temples dedicated to their many gods. They even had an altar to an unknown god. Paul then declared that Jesus was the God unknown to the Greeks, and he spoke about Jesus' life, death and resurrection.

The 'salt' in Paul's words made his speech palatable, and many people wanted to hear what he was talking about. When we season what we say and do with kindness and generosity, we can help others to know Jesus.

Prayer: *Dear heavenly Father, guide our words and actions so that they may bring others closer to you. Amen.*

Thought for the day: I can help people to meet Jesus through my words.

Carol Peter (Gujarat, India)

Walking with neighbours

Read Matthew 22:34–40

'You shall love the Lord your God with all your heart and with all your soul and with all your strength and with all your mind and your neighbour as yourself.'
Luke 10:27 (NRSV)

When I retired, I moved to the mountains and lived only a few miles from the Appalachian Trail. Each year, thousands set out to hike the entire trail – a months-long journey of nearly 2,200 miles. Hikers must carry everything they need to survive – for days at a time. Many hikers end up tired, sore, and short on water and food, despite their best planning.

Encountering these 'thru-hikers' on my day hikes, I was amazed at how they looked out for each other and shared their meagre resources. A few ounces of water, a little food, a bandage, an aspirin or a ride into town could make a huge difference. Strangers formed community. The other hikers became their new 'neighbours'.

As Christians, we are called to serve others and take care of our neighbours in need. On the trails I regularly visited, people benefitted from small kindnesses. I always brought extra food, supplies and a well-stocked first-aid kit on hikes. I was enriched by my interactions with hikers; we shared stories, laughed, hugged and prayed together. What opportunities do we have to serve others? Let us be observant and open-minded, pray about it and see what surfaces.

Prayer: *O God, our Saviour, thank you for the beauty of your world. We thank you for opportunities to meet new friends and neighbours. Amen.*

Thought for the day: Wherever I am, I can care for my neighbours and make a difference.

Chris Bullis (North Carolina, USA)

Out of my comfort zone

Read 2 Corinthians 12:1–10

*'My grace is sufficient for you, for my power is made perfect
in weakness.'*
2 Corinthians 12:9 (NIV)

As a Christian, I've always been intimidated by the concept of sharing out loud the word of God. My introverted personality made me uncomfortable at the thought.

However, while browsing for clothing in a store, a woman approached me and asked if I would help her decide on an outfit. She was going back to church and wanted to dress for the occasion. She seemed thankful for my help.

Her story was not unique. She had stepped away from her faith for a time, and now she feared being judged by church members. She was concerned that God was angry with her. I felt a connection with her. I seized the opportunity and shared a favourite scripture – 2 Corinthians 12:9. I also reminded her that Jesus paid the price for us all. Hearing two voices saying 'Amen' behind us, we turned to see two women listening intently to our conversation. I realised that amid the busyness around us we had just shared a spiritual moment. Both of us had taken a positive step in deepening our faith and trusting more in God. And we received no judgement, only loving support.

Prayer: *Dear Lord, give us the courage to share your word when the opportunity presents itself so that we can grow in our faith and bring hope to others. Amen.*

Thought for the day: Expressing my love for God
can encourage others.

Mary Ellen Hazen (Ohio, USA)

Dispel anxiety

Read Psalm 94:16–23

When my anxieties multiply, your comforting calms me down.
Psalm 94:19 (CEB)

One morning, I bent over and experienced an excruciating snap in my spine. My back locked up, leaving me in an awkward position, and I screamed in pain. Two weeks of pain, discomfort and limited mobility followed. When I experienced another intense pain, an MRI revealed multiple cracked and bulging disks, torn ligaments and compressed nerves.

As I stared at the test results, fear gripped my heart. Thoughts overwhelmed me: *I'll need surgery. I'll never walk well again. I'll have a permanent disability. I'll need to stay at home forever.*

Then I remembered Psalm 94:19, which I had read that morning. My head stopped spinning. My heart calmed. I trusted things would be okay. This scripture brought me peace, reminding me that God is aware of my anxieties.

Three years of tough step-by-step recovery followed. Amid painful experiences and frustration, scripture delighted my soul and enabled me to go on. Since then, whenever I'm overwhelmed, I recall Psalm 94:19. It brings me solace and redirects my attention from my problems to God. Through scripture, God continues to dissolve my anxieties.

Prayer: *Dear God, comfort us in our anxiety. Help us to trust that you are with us and that we are held in your love. Amen.*

Thought for the day: God's word in scripture has the power to overcome my anxieties.

Christel Owoo (Greater Accra, Ghana)

Keeping in touch

Read Hebrews 10:19–25

Don't stop meeting together with other believers, which some people have gotten into the habit of doing. Instead, encourage each other, especially as you see the day drawing near.
Hebrews 10:25 (CEB)

When I attended the 50-year reunion for my high school class, it was fun to reconnect with classmates I had not seen in decades. I chatted with two friends whom I had known since grade school. We promised to keep in touch after the reunion with monthly calls, weekly emails and exchanging Christmas cards. This continued for a while, but gradually contact became less frequent. Although we continue to exchange Christmas cards, our weekly and monthly communication has diminished.

This can also happen to our connection with God. Hebrews 10 admonishes believers to continue to worship and pray. Some members of the community to whom the letter was written had fallen out of touch. They had gotten out of the habit of regular meetings.

We can keep in touch with the Lord by gathering with other believers for regular Bible reading and study and to encourage one another. In a busy world, we don't have to fall out of touch with our faith.

Prayer: *Dear Lord, forgive us when we do not prioritise our connection with you and with other believers. Help us to keep our focus on you and encourage one another in faith. Amen.*

Thought for the day: Bible study and Christian fellowship help me remain connected to God.

Mike C. Bertoglio (Washington, USA)

Come to the table

Read Luke 14:15–23

Jesus replied: 'A certain man was preparing a great banquet and invited many guests. At the time of the banquet he sent his servant to tell those who had been invited, "Come, for everything is now ready."'
Luke 14:16–17 (NIV)

I love to watch the birds from my kitchen window. After refilling the feeder one day, I watched as a single bird arrived, grabbed a seed and flew off through the left side of the yard. Moments later, he returned, grabbed another seed and flew off again. Within minutes, the bird returned a third time and with him, all kinds of different birds arrived and shared a meal together. It looked like the first bird had sent out an invitation to all the neighbourhood to come to the table.

In the Bible, a table is a meeting place where God is present, and God's people gather. For Christians, the table represents the life and work of Jesus, reminding us that through the sacrament of Communion, we are marked as people of the new covenant. In Jesus we are loved by God and welcomed to the table just as we are. As followers of Christ, we are charged to extend an invitation to others in his name.

Prayer: *O God, thank you for the gift of your love and presence that we experience through Communion. Remind us always to extend an invitation to others who want to come to your table. Amen.*

Thought for the day: Christ sets a table and invites everyone to come.

Joy Fiesta (Pennsylvania, USA)

The two house builders

Read Matthew 7:24–27

'Everyone who hears these words of mine and puts them into practice is like a wise man who built his house on the rock.'
Matthew 7:24 (NIV)

When my mother passed away in 1982, I became an orphan and was raised in an environment without honesty or trust. With no firm foundation to rely on as a child, I needed guidance but did not know where to turn.

A few years after my mother's death I could feel that something was not right. I needed to choose how I would live my life – which path to follow. I started asking myself many questions: *Who am I? Where do I come from? Who is my father?* I asked my sisters, brothers and my aunts some of these questions, but there were no helpful answers.

I longed to have a father or someone to call 'father'. Because I was not raised by a family that believed in God, I didn't fully understand that God is our father who is in heaven. I started to seek God, going to church and praying with other people. Over time, God helped me to discover and understand who I am. I decided to accept God as my father. When we seek God, we can build a firm foundation of faith for a fulfilling life.

Prayer: *Dear heavenly Father, thank you for your love and guidance. Help us to seek you when our questions feel unanswerable, trusting that you are with us. Amen.*

Thought for the day: What am I doing to build a good relationship with God?

Khazamula Joseph Chauke (Gauteng, South Africa)

Capable

Read John 15:1–6

'I am the vine; you are the branches. If you remain in me and I in you, you will bear much fruit.'
John 15:5 (NIV)

My first sentence as a child was: 'I do it myself.' From the earliest years of my life, being fiercely independent has been part of my identity. It is a trait that is continually reinforced by our individualistic culture. I believed any problem could be solved with willpower and a self-help book. Over time, I have come to see that my aversion to asking for help and my tendency to strive to do things on my own stems from a lie. It's a lie that says people and maybe even Jesus will think less of me if I ask for help, a lie that says if I am not capable on my own, that I am a failure.

God's word in scripture, however, has shown me that we are not created to rely only on ourselves. Jesus said that he is the vine and we are the branches; that if a branch is not attached to the vine, it shrivels up and dies. When we strive to do everything on our own, we often fall short and end up frustrated and exhausted. Jesus invites us to keep company with him so that we can find the rest we need to live freely (see Matthew 11:28–30). When we stay close to Jesus, his strength lightens our burdens and enables us to flourish.

Prayer: *Dear heavenly Father, help us to remain close to you so that we may be filled with your love and joy. In Jesus' name. Amen.*

Thought for the day: Today I will humbly seek the help only Jesus can give.

Leah Tong (Ohio, USA)

The miracle of a seed

Read Matthew 13:18–23

Jesus said, 'Very truly I tell you, unless a grain of wheat falls to the ground and dies, it remains only a single seed. But if it dies, it produces many seeds.'

John 12:24 (NIV)

When travelling in northern Mexico, I have noticed that during late summer and early fall it is common to see large strings of chilli peppers, known as 'ristras', hanging from buildings and fences to dry. Ristras are an old tradition used to preserve the bright red chillies until they are needed. Some homes in the desert southwest of the United States now use these colourful chilli ristras as front porch decorations.

One spring day, a very old ristra hanging over my porch began to dry up and fall apart. Small, paper-thin chilli seeds were scattered everywhere. Most of these seeds blew away in the wind or fell to the rocks and gravel below, but a few seeds fell into my garden. With good soil and regular water, it did not take long for these old, dry seeds to sprout new chilli plants. Seeds that appeared to be dead quickly came to life in fertile soil. Those plants grew and produced many chilli peppers along with countless more seeds. What a miracle!

Like seeds in fertile ground, it takes only a few faithful believers sharing God's word to reach people who are receptive to Jesus' message of love. And when we provide continuing encouragement, we can nurture new communities of faith.

Prayer: *Faithful God, give us the courage to share your good news with others. In Jesus' name we pray. Amen.*

Thought for the day: Sharing God's word can yield miracles!

Doug Wingert (Arizona, USA)

A precious gift

Read Luke 1:26–38

*When the angel came to her, he said, 'Rejoice, favoured one!
The Lord is with you!'*
Luke 1:28 (CEB)

A few years ago, I was struggling with postpartum depression. I felt as though my life had veered off course; my ambitions stalled in the wake of motherhood, and I felt isolated.

Reflecting on that period, I recalled Luke 1:28, which sparked a profound shift within me and started my healing journey. Here was an angel sent by God, assuring Mary of divine favour as she faced the prospect of unwed motherhood. I realised that despite my circumstances, God was beside me, blessing me with the precious gift of motherhood.

I began to meditate on Luke 1:28 regularly, reminding myself that God had deemed me favoured and destined for blessings. The angel's message from God was not only to Mary but also to you and me: 'Rejoice, favoured one! The Lord is with you!'

Whatever challenges we face, God's favour surrounds us. Let us remain aware of and rejoice in God's presence and steadfast promises.

Prayer: *Loving God, thank you for your promises to us in scripture. Help us find solace in knowing that we are favoured, loved and blessed beyond measure. Amen.*

Thought for the day: I will cultivate a spirit of rejoicing, for I am favoured by God.

Lilian Okafor (Lagos, Nigeria)

On the merry-go-round

Read Psalm 46

God is not a God of disorder but of peace – as in all the congregations of the Lord's people.
1 Corinthians 14:33 (NIV)

When I was a child, I loved riding the merry-go-round. Watching the world spin by in a blur was fun. Getting dizzy and trying to walk a straight line after hopping off brought laughter from all my friends. Life was simple and easy.

Years later, as a husband and father of three girls, my life was often complicated and confusing – even with the joys of family, college and a new career. I sometimes felt overwhelmed by money worries and managing my family's busy schedules; and by concerns about war, economic downturns and political disagreements. Trying to keep up with the fast-paced spinning was no longer fun, and dizziness was no longer enjoyable.

Then I remembered something about riding a merry-go-round. At the edge, you move fast and things rush by. You have to hold on tight or be thrown off. At the centre, however, it is calm. In the same way, when life seems out of control, God is unaffected by the speed, challenges and complications of human life. God offers us a dependable and quiet refuge in a fast-changing and confusing world. Moving closer to God brings peace.

Prayer: *Dear God, when we feel out of control, remind us to put you at the centre of our lives. Help us to focus on you, our refuge, always. Amen.*

Thought for the day: God is a refuge from my fast-paced life.

Fred Reinhart (Michigan, USA)

Healing words

Read Proverbs 16:21–24

How good and pleasant it is when God's people live together in unity!
It is like precious oil poured on the head.
Psalm 133:1–2 (NIV)

The lock on the outside door of our tenement flat was sticking, making it difficult to turn the key. It would only open when the key was turned hard, which I could usually only do with my stronger right hand, making it awkward when I returned home carrying bags of shopping.

My sister took the oil can downstairs and lubricated the lock, and what a difference it made! The key now turned effortlessly, using either hand to operate it, and the door opened immediately!

It made me think of the words we use every day. Do we make life difficult for people or rub them up the wrong way because of our thoughtlessness, or do our words smooth situations and provide a film of loving-kindness which oils every interaction and brings joy to each situation? Even a few words spoken to a stranger at a bus stop may be meaningful and helpful in their time of need, and a few well-chosen words or an interjection of humour may defuse a potentially volatile situation.

As the Psalms show, God anoints us with the 'oil' of the Holy Spirit, that we may be a blessing to others through our words and actions.

Prayer: *Heavenly Father, may the words of our mouths and the meditations of our hearts be pleasing in your sight (see Psalm 19:14). Amen.*

Thought for the day: I will seek to build up those whom I meet through the words that I say.

Christine Hay (Scotland, United Kingdom)

In my weakness

Read Romans 8:18–28

We know that in all things God works for the good of those who love him, who have been called according to his purpose.
Romans 8:28 (NIV)

For a time I lived in a country far from my parents. My mother got sick and was hospitalised, then passed away after months of painful treatments. Unable to travel home, I supported my brother so he could travel to handle the funeral and care for our grieving father.

Two years later, our father had a stroke that left him unable to move or talk. I used up my savings to support my brother as he cared for our father. Then my brother had to be hospitalised for several months. Who would care for our father now?

I do not know how the story ends, but I know there is always the hope of God's salvation. I don't want others to be upset, so I rarely share the details of my life with any but my closest friends. But I trust that, in time, God's answers, provision and protection will turn this situation around. And if God's answers are different from what I hope and pray for, I will still praise God. I will boast of my weaknesses and hardships because in and through them, God works powerfully.

Prayer: *Lord Jesus, help us remember that you are with us even when we are weak and that you are our ever-present help in trouble. Amen.*

Thought for the day: When I am weak, Christ is strong.

Yana Ibragimova (North Gyeongsang Province, South Korea)

Gratitude for creation

Read Psalm 96

You made the heavens, even the highest heavens, and all their starry host, the earth and all that is on it, the seas and all that is in them. You give life to everything, and the multitudes of heaven worship you.
Nehemiah 9:6 (NIV)

One summer afternoon, we drove down the lane to our rural neighbourhood. We were surprised at what we saw in the grass by the road: a fox, a turkey and a deer within 50 feet of each other. In contrast to the fox's sleek form and shiny red fur, the turkey's body was out of proportion and jerked as it waddled along. Up ahead, the deer high-kicked majestically with its slender legs and long neck.

We were awed by the creative powers of our God. Although the three animals were different in every way, they were made by the same deity. Throughout creation, God's unique ingenuity is displayed. Yet, we're often oblivious to it and neglect to praise God for creation. Instead of being apathetic, I want to be more thankful and appreciative.

To accomplish these goals, I look for God's creative hand all around me – in the eyes of my friends and in the mysteries of God's universe. Then I make the effort to thank God in prayer.

Prayer: *Dear Lord, open our eyes to your beautiful creation, and put thanksgiving on our lips for the displays of your power. Amen.*

Thought for the day: God made everything and is worthy of praise.

Clint Eastman (Massachusetts, USA)

The beautiful, terrifying sea

Read Matthew 8:23–27

Jesus said to them, 'Bring some of the fish you have just caught.'
John 21:10 (NIV)

I am afraid of the sea. When I was three years old, I was walking along a beach in the winter with my dad, when I was knocked over by a freak wave. I was terrified! My dad swept me up in his arms, wrapped me in his duffle coat and carried me to the pier, where we warmed up with hot chocolate.

And yet I also love the sea. My son is a fisherman – the last thing I expected him to be – and he spends several days out at sea, at the mercy of the wind and the waves. (I pray each time he goes out.) Recently, he cooked me some fresh mackerel, and I hadn't realised how delicious freshly caught fish could be, or that fish like mackerel, with their rainbow scales, could be so beautiful.

Both aspects of the sea point me to the wonder of God. While the sea is vast and terrifying, especially during a storm, it is nevertheless still subject to God's command. With a word, Jesus stilled the sea, and when we are knocked down by life's waves, our heavenly Father scoops us up in his loving arms. The sea is also part of God's awesome creation, a source of wonder, beauty and blessing, which sustains many communities and on which many livelihoods depend.

Prayer: *Heavenly Father, thank you for the blessing of the oceans, as well as all your creation. May we be good stewards of your many gifts to us. Amen.*

Thought for the day: When we cry out to God in fear, he is near to help us.

Wendy Soane (England, United Kingdom)

Peace in troubled times

Read Psalm 34:15–22

The righteous person may have many troubles,
but the Lord delivers him from them all.
Psalm 34:19 (NIV)

As I faced a dangerous virus, fear took over. Every day felt like a struggle, and the idea of dying paralysed me. Medical help wasn't enough, so I turned to prayer.

While reading my Bible, I came across Psalm 34:19. This verse gave me comfort when fear tried to take over. Days were uncertain, but that verse was like a friend. I also started praying daily.

Unexpectedly, things started to improve. It wasn't a quick fix, but my fear started fading and so did my physical symptoms. Every day I got stronger, and the virus didn't have as tight a hold on me. I wasn't just getting better physically; it was like my faith was coming back, and I felt God's kindness.

Looking back, I'm grateful. Every breath used to remind me of fear, but now each one is a reminder of strength and hope. Psalm 34:19 now lives in my heart as a truth. This wasn't just about overcoming a virus; it was about finding faith and healing. In tough times, faith and prayer can be the lights that guide us. Psalm 34:19 is more than words; it's like a rope that pulled me out of the dark and into a new life.

Prayer: *Dear Lord, in our moments of struggle and brokenness, may we find solace in your attentive presence. Hear our cries, deliver us from troubles, and be our refuge. Amen.*

Thought for the day: The Lord is near to me in my brokenness.

Samuel E. (Ontario, Canada)

Quench your thirst

Read Ruth 2:8–12

'Whoever drinks the water I give them will never thirst.'
John 4:14 (NIV)

As I awoke in the predawn, I felt blessed to be lying beside my sleeping husband. I reflected on the special moments of our 62 years of marriage. We shared the joys of our wedding day and the births of three children. But we also shared our pain: crying together over the death of our infant daughter and the heartache we shared when our sons faced challenges. The highs and lows of our life together create a tapestry that covers and blesses our lives.

As is my habit when I wake early, I turned to scripture I have memorised. I thought about the story of Ruth. Boaz's kind words and offering of water caught my attention. It brought to mind Jesus' response to the Samaritan woman: 'Whoever drinks from the water that I will give will never be thirsty again. The water that I give will become in those who drink it a spring of water that bubbles up into eternal life' (John 4:14, CEB). The water Jesus spoke of refers to the Holy Spirit (see John 7:37–39).

This gave me peace and assurance that God's Spirit will support us through whatever lies ahead. There will surely be more challenges and more tears. But I know deep in my heart that God will quench my thirst.

Prayer: *Dear God, thank you for offering us the living water of your Spirit to refresh us on life's journey. Remind us to pause and drink each day. In Jesus' name. Amen.*

Thought for the day: I can endure life's challenges because the Holy Spirit sustains me.

Shirley Brosius (Pennsylvania, USA)

Decluttering

Read Luke 9:57–62

As they were walking along the road, a man said to him,
'I will follow you wherever you go.'
Luke 9:57 (NIV)

When my mother died, I received several boxes of her belongings. It was comforting to have some of the things that were special to her, but I needed to declutter and make space in my home for them. I spent an afternoon clearing out one room. Afterward, I was delighted to have room for the boxes as well as open space on my countertops and shelves. However, as weeks passed, I noticed the once-open spaces became cluttered all over again. To make room for anything new, I would need to declutter again.

In today's scripture reading, Jesus offered three people the opportunity to follow him – a precious gift that would require them to declutter their lives. Jesus explained that following him meant being willing to share in both the burdens and benefits of his life, prioritising his kingdom-building mission above all else. Jesus' words emphasised the importance of discipleship and helped his followers recognise who and what was keeping them from following Jesus fully.

What holds us back from following Jesus wholeheartedly? Jesus offers us the gift of himself – to share in his life and follow him every day. And with this comes the opportunity to declutter our lives to make more room for Jesus.

Prayer: *Dear Lord, help us to make more space in our hearts, minds and souls for the gift of your presence. Amen.*

Thought for the day: Today I will make more room in my life to follow Jesus.

Donyale Fraylon (Texas, USA)

God can be trusted

Read Psalm 42

Why are you cast down, O my soul, and why are you disquieted within me? Hope in God, for I shall again praise him, my help.
Psalm 42:5 (NRSV)

It was another usual workday in the 1990s that started with dropping my kids off at school and rushing to my office nearby. I was a member of the leadership team of a business during a turbulent time – the economy of the country was going downward, and I was stressed about meeting the financial commitments of the business.

As the first to enter the office, I noticed a letter in the fax machine that had been sent during the night. It contained the shocking news of the withdrawal of the main brand of products in our portfolio. It was an unexpected and most unwelcome message. The whole team was shocked, and during the following days many found alternative employment.

I was led to Psalm 42:5, where the psalmist resolves to put his hope in God. Though it was hard for me to trust at that time, given the circumstances, today I have seen that my trust was not in vain. God whom I trusted has guided me through the ups and downs to become the person that I am today. Though my aspirations did not materialise, God has moulded me and prepared me to become a useful vessel in God's hands.

Prayer: *Faithful God, we trust in you in all circumstances. Guide us through our valleys and lead us to the paths you want us to travel. Amen.*

Thought for the day: Even in the bleakest circumstances, I will trust God.

Rajkumar (Sri Lanka)

It's not about me

Read Galatians 6:7–10

Bear one another's burdens, and in this way you will fulfil the law of Christ.
Galatians 6:2 (NRSV)

My afternoon trip to the pool turned out to be anything but relaxing. A casual chat with a woman I didn't know evolved into a horrific account of her son's experiences with bullying at his school. He had been the victim of a vicious beating in a school bathroom. The story of this young teen's awful ordeal was deeply disturbing. I didn't want to hear the details, but I listened and tried to respond appropriately.

As I drove home trying to process what I had heard, I felt irritation that my relaxing afternoon had turned out to be a source of stress. As I was wishing I hadn't even gone to the pool, I thought of a Bible verse that shifted my perspective. God asks us to bear one another's burdens. God doesn't specify that those burdens be just those of the people we know and love; God just tells us to bear them.

Perhaps the woman just needed someone to help carry her heavy load because the end of summer and the return to school was a time of angst for both her and her son. I don't know nor do I need to know why she told me her story. God's ways are higher than our ways. The afternoon wasn't about me; it was about following God's command.

Prayer: *Dear God, when we want to run and hide from all the unsettling news in the world, may we pause to consider whether we can instead choose to stay and help. Amen.*

Thought for the day: I will help bear someone's burdens today.

Melanie S. Fretz (Pennsylvania, USA)

PRAYER FOCUS: THOSE WHO ARE BULLIED IN SCHOOL

Hidden beauty

Read Isaiah 45:1–7

I call you by your name; I give you a title, though you do not know me.
Isaiah 45:4 (NRSV)

I stepped out early one morning to take a walk. The damp sidewalk showed that it had recently rained. The sky was still dark as I started my usual two-mile loop, but it slowly brightened as I continued walking. At the end of my walk, as I rounded the corner towards home, I was surprised by a beautiful sight. Peeking out between the houses and trees was a rainbow. The dawn sky was a mix of blue and pink with a colourful rainbow in the middle.

As I stood there admiring the rainbow, a jogger approached from the opposite direction and went right by me without looking at the beautiful sight that I was witnessing. I then reflected on the countless times that I must have missed out on something wonderful that God had done.

God is always present and ready to show us something good, but we aren't always paying attention. It can be easy for us to go about our lives and forget that God is with us and loves and cares for us. I hope to be more mindful of God's constant presence, and I want to help shine the light of Christ in the lives of others.

Prayer: *Dear God, thank you for your presence and for the wonders of creation. Help us to shine your light so that others may experience your gifts of beauty and grace. Amen.*

Thought for the day: When I notice the beauty of God's presence, I will share it with others.

Rebecca L. T. Cho (Massachusetts, USA)

Help and healing

Read Psalm 118:1–7

When hard pressed, I cried to the Lord; he brought me into a spacious place.
Psalm 118:5 (NIV)

I was suffering from chest pain, having difficulty breathing and experiencing terrible headaches. My doctor prescribed an antibiotic and other medicines, but for a week I experienced nights with little sleep and coughing attacks that left me exhausted and crying. At the same time, an internal battle raged – anxiety, fear, disappointment and depressive moods attacked my mind and heart. *Does the Lord hear my prayers? Why am I not getting better? When can I leave this isolation and return to my normal life?*

But I continued asking the Lord for provision, help and healing. Psalm 118 assures us the Lord is with us and will help us when we cry out. This happened for me. Although my physical condition didn't improve for a couple more days, God sent people to pray for me, encourage me and provide for me. God gave my doctor wisdom in changing my treatment. And God gave me encouragement daily to feed my soul, providing a spacious place to breathe and persevere.

Eventually healing came, and joy and thankfulness flooded my heart again. It is painful to be in a hard place, feeling attacked from all sides. But with God, times of suffering can strengthen our faith and show us that God is faithful and trustworthy always.

Prayer: *Faithful Lord, we cry out to you, our helper. When illness and fear threaten to overwhelm us, give us courage to persevere. Amen.*

Thought for the day: The Lord helps me in my struggles.

Hadassah Treu (Pazardzhik, Bulgaria)

The kindness of others

Read Titus 3:1–8

By their fruit you will recognise them.
Matthew 7:20 (NIV)

I volunteer by delivering meals in my mountain community. After a major winter storm with single-digit temperatures and power outages, I drove up a steep, snow-covered road to check on an elderly woman who lived alone. When I saw snowmobile tracks leading to her house, I worried she might have had an emergency. I was relieved to find her healthy, content and warm beside a wood fire in her stove. When I asked about the tracks, she told me, 'Oh, some kid stopped by to check on me.' Even though she didn't know the person, she knew someone had made the effort to confirm she was safe.

I don't know who the snowmobiler was either, but on some level I feel that I do. This person's selfless act reflected the care, concern and grace our Lord shows us every day. We all are on a journey to our eternal home and, at one time or another, we all need a helping hand. As Jesus, our Saviour and Guide, said, 'Do you love me?… Take care of my sheep' (John 21:16). May each of us be ready to respond to those in need and be equally ready to accept the help others offer us.

Prayer: *Gracious God, thank you for the kindness we see in others, which is an extension of the grace and mercy you bestow on us. Amen.*

Thought for the day: Kindness extended to others
reflects the Lord's care.

Robert Boertien (Oregon, USA)

Embracing solitude

Read 1 Samuel 17:32–47

Your love, Lord, reaches to the heavens, your faithfulness to the skies. Your righteousness is like the highest mountains, your justice like the great deep. You, Lord, preserve both people and animals.
Psalm 36:5–6 (NIV)

When our family was considering getting a dog, my children promised to help with the care of the new puppy. Like many parents, I believed them. Twice a day I ended up walking our pup, Oatley, on a long leash in the pastures around our ranch. I was moody about the interruption to my schedule and lonely in the responsibility. Most days the wind would blow in my face and the ground was rough beneath my feet. Sometimes a hood over my head obscured the sky and birds. But I was surprised by the impact this time alone in nature had on me. God met me there.

King David spent his younger days in the pasture, tending sheep. Long hours of solitude surrounded by God's sweeping sky and rugged mountains formed thoughts and questions that shaped David's relationship with God that would serve him throughout his life.

I spent twelve months walking Oatley around the pastures. In the years following, my life took a new direction that I couldn't have predicted, and I went through a time of spiritual growth that amazed me. God had been making me ready for this new season.

Prayer: *Loving Father, help us to seek quiet places where we can hear your voice. Thank you for speaking to us. Amen.*

Thought for the day: Where can I seek a quiet moment with God today?

S. G. Beck (Oregon, USA)

Trusting God

Read Psalm 121
*'I have told you these things, so that in me you may have peace.
In this world you will have trouble. But take heart! I have overcome
the world.'*
John 16:33 (NIV)

I was going through a difficult and painful breakup. All my thoughts
focused on the rejection and loneliness I felt, and as a result I began to
suffer anxiety attacks. The pain and feelings of emptiness were deep,
and I thought nothing could assuage those feelings. But then I attended
a retreat sponsored by my local church and found Jesus. From that point
forward, everything changed. Jesus transformed my life and gave me the
assurance that I am not alone and that the way forward is to trust God.

Trusting God in moments of crisis challenges our faith. The cares
of the world often generate within us an anxiety that prevents us from
trusting God fully. The good news is that we, the children of God, know
that Jesus has overcome the world. To trust is to believe that God cares
and watches over us – that God is greater than any problem, illness or
crisis. God is the Creator of all. Whatever our situation, God loves us, God
supports us and God will help us see a way forward.

Prayer: *Heavenly Father, thank you for scripture that provides us the
assurance that we can find refuge in you. Rekindle our faith to trust
fully in your love. In the name of Jesus. Amen.*

Thought for the day: I choose to trust and believe the promises
in God's word.

Iván Esteban Arce Ibarra (Valle del Cauca, Colombia)

PRAYER FOCUS: PEOPLE SUFFERING FROM ANXIETY

Mind, body and spirit

Read 2 Timothy 3:10–17

All Scripture is God-breathed and is useful for teaching, rebuking, correcting and training in righteousness, so that the servant of God may be thoroughly equipped for every good work.
2 Timothy 3:16–17 (NIV)

Over the last 30 years, my nursing career has taken me from working twelve-hour shifts on my feet to an administrative role behind a desk. Over time, this more sedentary lifestyle has taken a toll on my physical and mental health. It became clear that I needed to incorporate a daily outdoor walk into my routine. Initially, I looked for any excuse I could think of to avoid these walks. Eventually though, I began looking forward to the fresh air and the sun on my face. My walks became one of the highlights of my day.

I recognised that being spiritually sedentary had similar effects. I had long been content to listen to sermons on Sunday then move through the rest of the week with little time spent studying the Bible or developing a personal relationship with Jesus. Just as a daily walk nourishes my body, my daily devotional time nourishes my spirit.

For many years now, my mother has provided every member of our family with the current issue of *The Upper Room*, either delivering it herself or posting it. These deliveries have played a huge role in my personal relationship with Jesus Christ. I have learned what my mother has known all along: nourishing our spirit is vital for our health.

Prayer: *Dear God, thank you for providing opportunities to stay close to you by studying your word. Thank you for the people who share your good news with the world. Amen.*

Thought for the day: I will take time to nourish my mind, body and spirit daily.

Laurie Smith (North Carolina, USA)

Hope from cut flowers

Read Psalm 13

'See, I am doing a new thing! Now it springs up; do you not perceive it?'
Isaiah 43:19 (NIV)

Less than a year after retirement I was diagnosed with cancer. I was shocked to realise my life might be significantly shorter than I expected. I had always taken good care of my body. Additionally, no one in my family has ever had cancer, and my mother is alive and well and in her late 80s. I couldn't understand why this was happening to me. I'm a faithful Christian. I've been able to participate in more activities at church since I retired. Was God done with me?

One day during this time of questioning, I purchased some cut flowers. I put them in a clear vase on my dining table where I could enjoy them. I didn't expect them to last long. Cut flowers may be attractive, but they usually die within a week. Imagine my surprise, however, when leafy buds began blooming on the flower stems even as the flowers on top began to die. As I drank my coffee one morning, it occurred to me that God was putting my mind at rest with the appearance of those leafy buds.

Like cut flowers, my lifespan may be shorter than I anticipated, but new growth can still happen while I'm dealing with cancer. Reconciled now to the situation I'm facing, I'm curious to see what God has planned for me.

Prayer: *Thank you, God, for reminding us that you bring new life to what may appear dead to us. Amen.*

Thought for the day: God can bring life to what I thought was dead.

Millie Thomas-Kearney (Washington, USA)

Free to be me

Read Exodus 14:1–18

'The Lord will fight for you, and you have only to keep still.'
Exodus 14:14 (NRSV)

I am a keyboardist and used to play every Sunday at a worship centre. I was very passionate about playing at church. However, as time went by I realised that some of my peers at church didn't appreciate my exuberance. As a result I started skipping church to avoid their unpleasant attitude towards me.

When I stopped playing in worship, it felt like I had cut my connection with God. But God sent my pastor to guide me to reconnect with our Lord. When I confided in my pastor regarding the challenges I experienced, he urged me to focus on what brings me to church and ignore what other people had to say.

Just as God set the people of Israel free from slavery in Egypt, God set me free from the judgement of others. From this experience, I learned that it is not about what people say or what you say about yourself; it's about what God wants for you. It is vital to serve God with honour and dignity.

Prayer: *Dear God, thank you for never forsaking us and loving us the way we are. Help us to joyfully fulfil our calling to serve you. Amen.*

Thought for the day: I will serve God with joy!

Bonginkosi Makgathulela (Gauteng, South Africa)

Open my eyes

Read Psalm 119:18–20

Open my eyes that I may see wonderful things in your law.
Psalm 119:18 (NIV)

As I neared the age of 62, I observed a marked decline in my night vision. I experienced blurred vision and sensitivity to light and its glare. My ophthalmologist explained that I had developed cataracts – a condition affecting the eye that causes clouding of the lens. If not treated, it leads to a gradual progression of vision problems that may result in vision loss. After some hesitation and much prayer, I opted to go ahead with cataract surgery on my left eye. When the patch was removed from my eye after surgery, I was amazed at how well I could see. I have since had surgery on my right eye as well.

Psalm 119:18 has reminded me that there are times when I may need the Lord to correct my spiritual vision as well. Just as my physical vision became dull over time, my spiritual vision can also become blurred when I fail to talk to God or spend time studying God's word regularly. Like the surgeries on my physical eyes, having my spiritual vision corrected can enable me to see both the good and the not-so-good parts of my life of faith. May God open our eyes and renew our spiritual vision so that we can see clearly what God has for us to do.

Prayer: *Most holy God, help us to see the wonderful promises in your word and the blessings you bring into our lives every day. Amen.*

Thought for the day: God's word can open my eyes to God's purpose for me.

Betty White Coleman (Mississippi, USA)

Trusting God's plan

Read Jeremiah 29:10–13

'Do not worry about tomorrow, for tomorrow will worry about itself. Each day has enough trouble of its own.'
Matthew 6:34 (NIV)

In the months after my wife's death, anticipation has deepened my grief. Special occasions and traditions established over 50 years of marriage – birthdays, anniversaries, holidays – loom like dark walls hiding everything beyond. As each date approaches, I pray, 'God, how do I endure this?'

God has helped me through the first few of these occasions, and now I see how worrying about future pain just makes present pain worse. This helps me face the most painful challenge of all: how I'll spend the rest of my life without my wife.

The Jewish exiles in Babylon must have felt something similar after being displaced from their homeland. Facing an unclear future in a strange place must have been terrifying. But Jeremiah assured them that God had a plan for them to thrive and to remain connected to their creator. They just needed to be patient, make the best of present circumstances and trust God.

I find immense comfort in Jeremiah's words to the exiles. I don't know what a future without my wife will be like. But I can trust God today and let the future worry about itself. I know I can rely on God's plan – whatever it is, for however much time remains.

Prayer: *Thank you, Lord, for giving us hope in our darkest moments with your assurance that you know the plan you have for us and that it is good. Amen.*

Thought for the day: I will trust God's plan for me.

Bob Tippee (Texas, USA)

Hold and step

Read Matthew 14:25–31

My soul clings to you; your right hand upholds me.
Psalm 63:8 (NRSV)

The youngest member of our family was learning to go up and down our very steep front steps on her own. As she made her way up and down, whoever was with her would remind her to keep a tight grip on the handrail, saying, 'Come on, Laila! Hold tight and step.'

Some time later, after a lengthy hospital stay, I came home and was still very unsteady on my feet. As I stood hesitating at the top of the steps, a little voice piped up, 'It's all right, Grandma. Just hold and step.' She kept on encouraging me until I reached the ground.

What a wonderful life lesson! We may not be floundering in deep water as Peter was in Matthew's gospel, but whenever we are experiencing trouble, fear or weakness, all we need to do is firmly grasp God's hand and move forward in faith. Out of great love for us, God will provide the strength that we lack.

Prayer: *Dear Lord, thank you for your love and grace. Remind us that when we reach out in faith, you will always be there to help and sustain us. We pray as Jesus taught us, 'Our Father which art in heaven, Hallowed be thy name. Thy kingdom come. Thy will be done, as in heaven, so in earth. Give us day by day our daily bread. And forgive us our sins; for we also forgive every one that is indebted to us. And lead us not into temptation; but deliver us from evil'* (Luke 11:2–4, KJV). Amen.

Thought for the day: God gave me this day; how can I best use this gift?

Jean Warner (New South Wales, Australia)

Enjoy the journey

Read Romans 5:1–5

We also glory in our sufferings, because we know that suffering produces perseverance; perseverance, character; and character, hope.
Romans 5:3–4 (NIV)

When I was a young child, I had no concept of time. On car trips I would often ask my parents, 'Are we there yet?' It didn't matter if we were going down the street or to a place far away. I was so excited to get to the destination that I didn't take the time to enjoy the journey.

We often ask God the same question: *Are we there yet?* We want to know when we will get to the destination we desire. The journey can seem long. Sometimes it's boring. Sometimes it's difficult. Sometimes it's worrisome. And sometimes it's painful. However, it's in the process of the journey that God shapes our character. Each day is a gift from God in which we can commune with our creator and discover our God-given purpose.

Sometimes it's difficult to keep going, but God builds us up and strengthens us along the way. We don't need to rush the process. We can trust God's timing and appreciate each step along the way.

Prayer: *Dear God, when we feel anxious and impatient, calm our spirits and focus our minds on you. Amen.*

Thought for the day: I will trust in God's timing and celebrate each step of my journey.

Tomeka B. Scales (Maryland, USA)

All part of the story

On the flight home from a holiday out west, my seatmate asked me what I do for a living. When I told her, she said she knew *The Upper Room* well because her grandmother was a longtime reader. This is not an uncommon experience. Someone asks me about my job, I tell them and they go on to talk about their connection to *The Upper Room*.

I would be lying if I said I don't love these interactions. They remind me that my work has value and that I am part of something with a reach that extends far beyond what I'm actively thinking about each day. It began long before me and will hopefully continue long after I'm gone.

The magazine you hold in your hands goes back several decades – nine to be exact. This year, 2025, we celebrate our 90th year of publication. The story of our origin and subsequent history is varied, full and rich. And it all started with a mustard seed. Frances Craig, a member of a Methodist church in San Antonio, Texas, and Dr Grover Emmons, a preacher with all the right connections, recognised the need for a devotional resource for daily home use. Through their hard work, prayer and ingenuity, they made it happen. The inaugural issue was already at the printer when Dr Emmons got the idea for the name of the new magazine while listening to a sermon on the upper room and the events of Pentecost from Acts 1 and 2.

The first issue went to press in 1935 with a print run of 100,000 copies. We were soon printing half a million copies, and the number continued to grow. While we've made small changes to the size and format over the years, the core attributes of the magazine remain unchanged – the daily pattern of prayer and meditation, ordinary people sharing their faith stories and the devotional guide's global character.

In the years since, we've grown to more than 30 language editions in over 100 countries around the world. *The Upper Room* has survived, among other challenges, wars, a national paper shortage, significant shifts in the publishing industry and a global pandemic.

In the decades since our founding, our vision has expanded beyond the daily devotional guide to include other magazines, book publishing and programmes. Some of our offerings have changed with demand and the spiritual needs of the community we serve. In addition to the daily devotional guide, our current resources include Upper Room Books, The Academy for Spiritual Formation, Walk to Emmaus, Face to Face, Journey to the Table and The Center for Healing and Resilience.

While our roots are in the Methodist church, our content and mission are ecumenical, and we work hard to remain true to the biblical story from which we take our name. *The Upper Room* is a place where everyone, in all our God-given variety and diversity, can gather to share experiences of how God is working in our lives.

There's more to the story of *The Upper Room*. A lot more. If you want to explore our history in greater depth, I recommend reading *Where the World Meets to Pray: People and Stories of The Upper Room* by Mary Lou Redding (Upper Room Books). I read it about once a year to ground myself in my work and place in *The Upper Room*'s ministry.

Why am I telling you all this? I think it's for the same reason that I feel a sense of (holy?) pride when someone on a plane shares a memory of *The Upper Room* or, even better, tells me that they read it every day – to remind me that I am a small part of something that is much larger than myself, a story that started almost a century ago and continues on. You are part of that story too, and I do this work for you. It wouldn't mean much if you weren't on the other end. Thank you for being there. Once the magazine is out in the world, I don't always think about where it goes or what it does. If and when our paths cross, I hope you will tell me about it.

QUESTIONS FOR REFLECTION

1 When have you contributed to an event, community or mission that connected to something larger than yourself? What inspired you about that experience? Why was that experience important to you?

2 Who in your community serves in a way that makes a meaningful difference in the lives of others? How will you express your gratitude and show support for them?

Andrew Garland Breeden, senior editor

Confidently me

Read 2 Corinthians 3:12–18
We all, who with unveiled faces contemplate the Lord's glory, are being transformed into his image with ever-increasing glory, which comes from the Lord, who is the Spirit.
2 Corinthians 3:18 (NIV)

For years, I lived in fear of what people would think of me if they really knew me. Everyone else seemed to know the Bible better, pray more and know how to speak church language better than I could. I worried that I would lose the respect of my friends, especially my Christian friends. This lack of confidence transferred to my everyday life, and I was afraid to be myself.

I asked God to help me overcome this feeling of inadequacy. As I read the Bible, I came to realise that God loves me and forgives me. I truly began to believe that I was who God created me to be. I wasn't ashamed anymore; I was the daughter of the king!

My new attitude helped me become confident in who I was, and I began to live in a more open and honest way. Living confidently as a Christian means reflecting Jesus and acknowledging you are a child of the living God. When we allow the love of Jesus to transform our self-image, God's light can shine through us for others to see.

Prayer: *Creator God, thank you for loving, forgiving and empowering us. Help us to live in a way that shows your love clearly to the world around us. Amen.*

Thought for the day: I can have confidence because I am a child of God.

Adena H. Paget (Alberta, Canada)

Blessings unrealised

Read Romans 8:26–28

We know that in all things God works for the good of those who love him, who have been called according to his purpose.
Romans 8:28 (NIV)

I first noticed something was wrong with my oldest sister when she was 65 years old. I received a thank-you card for her retirement gift and didn't recognise her handwriting. That was the first sign of her dementia, followed by many inexplicable decisions she would make in the coming years.

Our family worried about her living alone. She could no longer drive, shop for groceries or do her own laundry. She refused to go to the doctor. When she had a stroke and got weaker, she was no longer able to care for herself. We moved her into a care facility. This was the same home our mother had moved to when she was of sound mind at age 93. And now my sister was living there. She was just 73.

In my heartbreak, I asked God to help me see some good in this situation. Soon God helped me accept my sister's dementia and showed me the blessings we had all been given. I realised that my sister was now in a clean, warm place, receiving nourishing meals, and cared for by a kind staff. She got medical attention when she needed it, and we no longer had to worry about her living alone. My sadness for my sister had made me overlook God's blessings, but I received comfort when I recognised how faithfully God had blessed her and us.

Prayer: *Dear heavenly Father, when life is hard and sadness overwhelms us, remind us of your promise that with you all things work for our good because of your love for us. Amen.*

Thought for the day: On my hardest days, God's presence can bring me comfort and peace.

Denise Robson (Michigan, USA)

God's signet ring

Read 1 Peter 2:4–10

'I will take you, O Zerubbabel my servant, son of Shealtiel, says the Lord, and make you like a signet ring; for I have chosen you.'
Haggai 2:23 (NRSV)

The book of Haggai – one of the so-called minor prophets – is not a well-known or oft-cited part of the Bible, but I was struck by this promise that it makes – that we are chosen of God! To illustrate how precious we are to God, Haggai uses the image of a signet ring.

Signet rings are used to impress a mark or seal, often in hot wax to secure a letter or validate a document. In the days when few people could read or write, it was the equivalent of signing one's name to guarantee their word. The ring was engraved with a reverse image of the seal, so that when stamped on the wax it would give a positive image.

While Haggai is specifically addressing the governor of Judah, as the letter of 1 Peter says, we too are God's 'chosen people' and 'special possession' (1 Peter 2:9)! We can replace 'Zerubbabel' with our own name in Haggai's promise and know that God wants to use us to leave a mark on the world that reflects God's image.

To push the metaphor further, I don't doubt that, if it could feel, a signet ring would find the process of being engraved painful. Likewise, being formed into the image of God may at times be a painful process. But, as Peter goes on to say: 'if you suffer as a Christian, do not be ashamed, but praise God that you bear that name' (1 Peter 4:16, NIV).

Prayer: *Dear Lord, thank you that you have chosen us. Help us to accept even the hard experiences of life as an opportunity to grow more like you. Amen.*

Thought for the day: I bear the name of Christ.

Hilary Hartley (England, United Kingdom)

At the feet of Jesus

Read Psalm 103:1–12

Be kind and compassionate to one another, forgiving each other,
just as in Christ God forgave you.
Ephesians 4:32 (NIV)

Recently, a friend of my son came to visit us. He is an officer in the Indian army. As he came in he greeted everyone. When my son introduced me as his mother, his friend came to touch my feet. In keeping with an ancient Indian tradition, young people often greet their teachers and elders by touching their feet as a mark of respect and to receive a blessing.

Luke's gospel records the story of a sinful woman anointing Jesus' feet with costly perfume (see Luke 7:36–50). Her action drew criticism from the people: does Jesus not know what kind of woman this is?

I wonder how we would have responded. Do we feel more deserving of God's grace than those rejected by society? Jesus extended grace and forgiveness to everyone, including those forgotten by society. In fact Jesus lauded this woman's extravagant act of love as an anointing and blessed her. She found consolation, acceptance and respect at Jesus' feet. Not only that, but she received forgiveness.

Are we willing to extend grace and respect to those who have been rejected and judged by family or society? Before we answer, we need only think of the grace and love we receive from Jesus.

Prayer: *God of grace and mercy, help us to love and forgive one another as you love and forgive us. In Jesus' name. Amen.*

Thought for the day: God's love and faithfulness should lead me to love and respect God's people.

Navamani Peter (Karnataka, India)

Be confident

Read Exodus 4:10–16

'Now go; I will help you speak and will teach you what to say.'
Exodus 4:12 (NIV)

While travelling for missions in South America, I struggled to learn a new language. I had no confidence when it came to communicating, but I pushed myself, knowing the Lord wanted me to share the good news with others.

However, one time when a young woman asked me to lead her in a prayer of confession and commitment, I almost gave up because my Spanish was so bad. I told her that I was going to find someone else to help her, but she shook her head in protest. She told me that she understood me completely and that she was ready to accept Jesus into her life. The Holy Spirit had been at work between us in spite of my feelings of inadequacy about my language skills. I didn't have to be fluent for God to make a difference. I needed only the willingness to be a channel for God and to be confident in God's ability.

I can empathise with Moses' hesitation at God's command for him to go to Pharaoh and ask for the Israelites' freedom (see Exodus 3:7–11). In today's scripture reading, Moses insisted that he was not eloquent enough for such a mission, and he felt that God should send someone else. When I became a Christian, I realised that God is with me wherever I am, and the assurance God gave Moses also extends to all of us.

Prayer: *Dear Father, you are able to do far more than we can even imagine. Help us to speak up and share your goodness with others whenever we have the opportunity. Amen.*

Thought for the day: Today I will speak about my faith and trust God with the results.

Deborah Meroff (Maine, USA)

Depend on God's word

Read John 4:4–14

Jesus said to her, 'Everyone who drinks of this water will be thirsty again, but those who drink of the water that I will give them will never be thirsty. The water that I will give will become in them a spring of water gushing up to eternal life.'
John 4:13–14 (NRSV)

I bought a succulent for my weekly Bible study group to show my appreciation for all that I am learning about God's word and applying it to my daily life. We keep the plant on a bookshelf in the classroom where we meet. The succulent also serves as a reminder of our dependence on God. It depends on the water it is given, and it stores the water in its stems to be used as needed until the next watering.

Isn't that like what we do with scripture? When we regularly spend time studying the Bible, we are sustained by the word of God. If we are wise, we store up God's word to cling to in any circumstance.

God is always present to quench our spiritual thirst. When we cling to God and God's word, we are able to rely on God in challenging times and praise God in good times.

Prayer: *Dear God, thank you for quenching our spiritual thirst with your word and for sustaining us with your love. Amen.*

Thought for the day: I will store up God's word to help me in spiritually dry times.

Dennis G. Moore (Iowa, USA)

Holding on to God

Read Isaiah 41:9–13

*I am the Lord your God, who grasps your strong hand, who says
to you, Don't fear; I will help you.*
Isaiah 41:13 (CEB)

My granddaughter is just over one year old. She is standing and taking
tentative steps but has not yet tried to walk on her own. When she wants
to move from one spot to another, instead of crawling, she will look around
for someone she trusts and hold out her hand. If one of us responds to
her, offering her our hand, she will use it to steady herself as she stands
and then will walk with us to where she wants to go. She doesn't walk
anywhere without holding on to the hand of someone stronger and
steadier than herself.

It is a wonderful thing to know that we don't have to walk through
life alone. Whether we feel confident or unsure, brave or fearful, joyful or
sorrowful, God is always with us, strong and steady for us to hold on to.

We can always reach out for God whose guidance, understanding
and protection are always there for us. God wants to walk with us at all
times. Just like my granddaughter will take my hand in trust, knowing
that I love her, we too can hold on to God, trusting God's steadfast love
to keep us from falling.

Prayer: *Dear God, thank you for loving us and for your steadying
presence that holds us up and helps us along whatever path life takes.
Amen.*

Thought for the day: God holds me through good times and bad.

Joy Margetts (Wales, United Kingdom)

Always thankful

Read Psalm 100
Give thanks to him; bless his name.
Psalm 100:4 (NRSV)

I am a big fan of thank-you notes. I like sending them; I like receiving them; I even keep a file of the thank-you notes I have received over the years.

One of my favourite notes came from a former parishioner. It was handwritten in her beautiful script on an ivory-coloured card embossed with her initials. She was thanking me for taking the time to meet with the community organisation she helped lead – an organisation that was close to her heart. She also offered some kind words about the brief meditation on gratitude I had shared that night. 'It is so easy,' she wrote, 'to take our many blessings for granted, as you pointed out. Yesterday I stopped to think about some of the things I have to be thankful for. Thanks for reminding me.'

God has given us so much to be thankful for. But sometimes, like children caught up in the excitement of receiving new toys, we forget to give thanks. Psalm 100 tells us that God made us and watches over us like a shepherd watches over sheep. How truly blessed we are!

Prayer: *Generous God, you have given so much to us! Keep us ever mindful of that reality. Thank you for your love, care and presence in our lives. Amen.*

Thought for the day: Today I will thank God for my blessings.

John H. Danner (Florida, USA)

Three crosses

Read Mark 8:34–37

May I never boast of anything except the cross of our Lord Jesus Christ, by which the world has been crucified to me and I to the world.
Galatians 6:14 (NRSV)

'Christ has died. Christ is risen. Christ will come again.' This familiar refrain from the Communion liturgy frames the story of our faith.

In my little church, there are three crosses on display that differ in style but together symbolise this message for me. One cross is placed on the altar. It is made of metal and painted a dark gold colour that makes me think of Jesus' death on the cross – 'Christ has died.' An illuminated cross hangs above the altar. Seeing it, I think of the resurrection – 'Christ is risen.' The third cross, found in the stained-glass window behind the altar, is encircled by a crown. To me, this speaks of Jesus' return, and I think of the church proclaiming his coming kingdom – 'Christ will come again.'

I don't know if this arrangement of the crosses is intentional, and I don't know if anyone else in the congregation sees them the way I do. However, looking at the crosses before the service starts and reflecting on this interpretation helps me to prepare for worship. God's love is all around us, and we can find reminders of God's unending love when we take the time to look.

Prayer: *Loving God, help us to notice your presence around us. Thank you for reminders of what you have done and will do for us. In Jesus' name. Amen.*

Thought for the day: What symbols and images remind me of God's love?

Reg Rice (Pennsylvania, USA)

Blessed to give

Read 2 Corinthians 8:1–5

The Lord Jesus himself said: 'It is more blessed to give than to receive.'
Acts 20:35 (NIV)

In the rental house where my family and I used to live, there was space on the second floor for us to grow potted plants. My sister and I planted pandanus, aloe vera, chilli peppers, snake fruits, dragon fruits and other plants. However, we had to move from that house because the owner was going to renovate it.

Our new rental house didn't have space for our potted plants. My sister was sad, feeling her efforts had been in vain. We ended up giving the plants to friends and neighbours. I said to my sister, 'In this time, God gave us the opportunity to share.' Everyone rejoiced when they received the plants from us, which made us happy.

Even when our gifts are simple, they can bring joy to others, and the act of giving brings joy to us. That is why Jesus said, 'It is more blessed to give than to receive.' And that is why the Macedonians in today's scripture reading pleaded for the privilege of sharing in the service to the Lord's people (see 2 Corinthians 8:4). I imagine they said, 'We don't want to miss the opportunity!' God's heart is pleased when we give. Like the Macedonians, my sister and I were grateful for this opportunity from God to give.

Prayer: *Dear God, open our eyes to see every opportunity that you have given us to show generosity to others. Amen.*

Thought for the day: Today I will look for opportunities to give to others.

Linawati Santoso (East Java, Indonesia)

Making all things new

Read 2 Corinthians 5:16–21

He who was seated on the throne said, 'I am making everything new!'
Revelation 21:5 (NIV)

There are many beautiful stained-glass windows in Hereford Cathedral that depict people and stories from the Bible. Some are centuries old and served as visual aids for the congregations; others are more modern, such as the Thomas Traherne Windows in the Audley Chapel.

There is one window, however, above the doorway to the cathedral shop, that is often overlooked. Unlike all the others it is made from stained glass that has been recovered from other broken windows. As a result, it is a mishmash without obvious design. One part depicts the sun, moon and planets in a dark blue sky, perhaps taken from a window originally portraying the creation story. The rest is a jumble of colours, with fragments of saints, knight's armour and sections of script. Who-ever decided to save the glass and to create something new was surely an early recycler who found new artistic abstract expression that still communicates with us.

Some years ago, the then dean of the cathedral told me he thought this window is a metaphor for our lives. Like the dean, I believe God picks up all the brokenness in all the damaged places of our lives. He is able to rework and remake us into something beautiful that can communicate God's loving presence to others.

Prayer: *Dear Lord, thank you for those who restore and make stained-glass windows that speak of God's love. Amen.*

Thought for the day: I am part of God's new creation.

Faith Ford (England, United Kingdom)

Grace in sorrow

Read Exodus 16:11–19

He said to me, 'My grace is sufficient for you, for power is made perfect in weakness.'
2 Corinthians 12:9 (NRSV)

I had worked in ministry for a while and had been a counsellor, spending countless hours surrounded by others' grief. But it was a whole new experience when my mother died and grief came home with me. Grief sat on my couch, pulled up a chair at my dinner table, lay in my bed and followed me to the bathroom. I had to learn about grief by living with it.

Grief has been a demanding teacher. I have never felt such sorrow. There are depths of loss that no human comfort can reach. Grief is isolating in this way.

But here is the strangest thing I have experienced through all of this: I have never felt such hope! In those depths of sorrow, where no one else could go, I communed with Jesus Christ. Christ met me in ways that I had never known before. I discovered that his grace really is sufficient. Like manna in the desert, his grace is enough for today. It is enough for this moment, but I cannot store it up for future moments. I have to trust that the grace of Christ will meet me every day for as long as I wander through any desert. And so far, every time, grace has been with me – and it has been enough.

Prayer: *Dear God, thank you for walking with us through the depths of sorrow. We trust that you will go with us through every circumstance. Amen.*

Thought for the day: God is always with me in my grief.

Brittany Ison (Ohio, USA)

Restore me, Lord!

Read 2 Chronicles 24:1–14

After you have suffered for a little while, the God of all grace, who has called you to his eternal glory in Christ, will himself restore, support, strengthen and establish you.

1 Peter 5:10 (NRSV)

The small, dilapidated house I bought was a dream come true. For 15 years I had told my husband that if I had some extra money, I would buy an old house, renovate it and rent it out. Now I had the opportunity! I planned a complete remodel for the house and employed skilled labourers of all trades to do the work. I felt like King Joash from today's scripture reading who decided to restore the house of the Lord.

The workers installed new windows, doors, electrical wiring, plumbing and flooring, along with new fixtures and cabinetry for the kitchen and bathroom. When the work was done, the little house was unrecognisable from its former self. Even the appraiser was astonished to see how the once run-down property had been transformed by the changes.

God wants to transform our lives in much the same way. Perhaps we have weathered difficult relationships, economic hardship or a debilitating illness. There is always hope in believing that our gracious God is able to turn our situation around. No matter the condition or circumstances we may find ourselves in, God's plan is to renew and restore us.

Prayer: *Merciful God, thank you for seeing our true value through Jesus Christ. Help us to trust that you are at work in our lives. Amen.*

Thought for the day: With God, I am never beyond repair.

Arlene Timber-Henry (Caribbean Netherlands)

God's timing

Read Lamentations 3:19–26

The Lord is good to those whose hope is in him, to the one who seeks him; it is good to wait quietly for the salvation of the Lord.
Lamentations 3:25–26 (NIV)

Our oldest grandson, Amadeo, was on his way home from a visit with friends in another state. Anticipating his brother's return, Alex, our 14-year-old grandson, began sending group texts to the whole family with his newly acquired phone: 'Are you here yet, Amadeo? How about now? Now? Now?' All of our phones began pinging. While Alex was having fun with his new phone, the rest of us were rolling our eyes at the constant messages.

Sometimes my prayers are a lot like Alex's texts, but the questions are more serious. I ask God: 'When are you going to fix things and bring evil to justice and give us peace? How about now? Now? Now?'

In today's scripture from Lamentations, the prophet Jeremiah shares what God had taught him after the destruction of Jerusalem. There had been no miraculous rescue for God's people. Many soldiers had been killed, people had starved from famine, and thousands had been marched off as slaves (see Jeremiah 52). And yet, God showed Jeremiah that God's faithful love had not ended and 'God's compassion isn't through'.

When it comes to prayer, we may have certain expectations about how God should respond and when. But God's goodness and salvation have no time limits. No matter what, we can trust that God's timing is better than ours.

Prayer: *Father God, in all circumstances, teach us to trust as we wait for you. Amen.*

Thought for the day: I will trust in God's perfect timing.

Peter Caligiuri (Florida, USA)

The words we speak

Read Ephesians 4:29–32

Avoid godless chatter, because those who indulge in it will become more and more ungodly.
2 Timothy 2:16 (NIV)

One of my former co-workers had frequent outbursts of anger in the workplace – throwing papers, muttering curse words and lashing out at others. As recipients of such behaviour, another co-worker and I began talking negatively about her. For weeks we grumbled together about this co-worker.

Then one afternoon, as I began to complain about a recent outburst I had observed, my friend cut me off and said, 'I'm sorry, but I don't want to speak negatively about her anymore.' My surprise quickly turned to embarrassment. My friend's comment made me realise that I had been participating in workplace gossip. We agreed to refrain from speaking negatively about our co-worker and instead focused on her many wonderful qualities.

While talking about a co-worker or complaining about our boss may seem innocent at first, the byproducts of such talk are far from innocent. Seeds of resentment, bitterness and anger begin to sprout in our hearts when we engage in such talk.

While the transition from speaking negative words to uplifting words about my co-worker didn't change her behaviour or prevent future outbursts, it changed my heart and gave me a greater sense of contentment and joy.

Prayer: *Dear God, help me to guard my tongue and refrain from engaging in conversations that spread negativity or strife. Amen.*

Thought for the day: The words I speak shape the way I view the world.

Emily C. Marszalek (Idaho, USA)

God is close

Read Mark 4:35–41

He arose, and rebuked the wind, and said unto the sea, Peace, be still. And the wind ceased, and there was a great calm.
Mark 4:39 (KJV)

First I heard a thud and then a cry. My three-year-old son had slipped on our wet balcony floor. When I checked on him, I saw a gaping wound beside his right eye. In the emergency room, the doctor said he would need two stitches. My son began to cry. He reached for me and tried to get up. As his mother, I knew what to do. While the nurses held his head still, I softly sang 'Jesus loves me', his favourite song, into his left ear. He relaxed and the doctor was able to complete the procedure.

This experience made me recall how Jesus calmed the storm in Mark 4 by speaking to the waves. When all seemed hopeless, Jesus' words pacified not only the troubled waters but also the disciples' fearful hearts. Just as Jesus was with the disciples in the storm, God is close to us during the storms of our lives. When the waves are high, God's voice can be our soothing song. We can find rest in God's arms.

Just as my son needed my comforting words and presence so that the doctor could work, we can rely on God's word and presence to still us as God works in our lives to stitch together carefully the broken pieces, enabling us to heal, grow and glorify God.

Prayer: *Dear Father, thank you that you are with us during the hardships we face. Help us to trust in your presence. Amen.*

Thought for the day: During life's storms, I will focus on God's word.

Ruthie Solitario (Bulacan, Philippines)

Cleaning the closet

Read Isaiah 43:16–21

'See, I am doing a new thing! Now it springs up; do you not perceive it? I am making a way in the wilderness and streams in the wasteland.'
Isaiah 43:19 (NIV)

I had not cleaned out my closet in years, and it had become a time capsule of the various stages of my life. Here were the business suits I had worn decades ago as a professional. When I wore them I felt dressed for success. They still fit, but I now had no opportunities to wear them. And there on the shelf was a carry-on suitcase my late husband, Jerry, had used on many trips. I had my own luggage, so why was I keeping his? I had so many other more personal items to remind me of our years together.

It had been 15 years since I retired, and almost a decade had passed since Jerry died. Yet I was still holding on to many vestiges of my past. I knew I needed to clear out the closet and make room for new things.

Scripture tells us: 'Do not dwell on the past.' Keeping unneeded clothes or luggage wasn't likely to hurt me. But clearing the closet made me wonder: *Have I been holding on to memories and habits that keep me from fully pursuing the new things God has planned for me?* I pray that God will help me embrace the future God has in store for me.

Prayer: *Eternal God, help us to accept with confidence and gratitude the plans you have for us. In Jesus' name. Amen.*

Thought for the day: What do I need to let go of to make room for God's new things in my life?

Lisa Stackpole (Wisconsin, USA)

Led by God

Read Mark 10:46–52

Trust in the Lord with all your heart, and do not rely on your own insight. In all your ways acknowledge him, and he will make straight your paths.

Proverbs 3:5–6 (NRSV)

I enjoy taking early morning runs, and before I leave the house, I check the weather conditions from the nearby airport. One morning, the visibility at the airport was down to one mile. A thick layer of grey clouds hung above the treetops. As I ran, I heard a plane overhead, but due to the cloud cover I couldn't see it, and I knew that the pilots couldn't see the ground either. Pilots must always rely on their training and sophisticated instruments to safely fly and land the plane, but this is especially true when visibility is reduced.

Sometimes I struggle to see where I need to go in life. I lose focus, and finding my way is difficult. In those moments, I work to regain my bearings with the words from Proverbs 3:5–6.

Trusting in God is not always easy. Yet that is exactly what Bartimaeus did when he asked Jesus to restore his sight; he trusted God in his heart. On days when the way is unclear, my heart needs to be more trusting, just like Bartimaeus.

Prayer: *Faithful God, help our hearts to trust you when our vision is clouded. Guide us through your word. Amen.*

Thought for the day: When the way seems unclear, I will trust God to lead me.

Bill Pike (Virginia, USA)

The appropriate time

Read Psalm 40:1–5

I waited patiently for the Lord; he inclined to me and heard my cry.
Psalm 40:1 (NRSV)

In my country, it is common to see drivers constantly change lanes to get ahead of others, trying to reach their destination a bit quicker. Sometimes, though, after changing lanes it seems that the drivers in the other lane are moving ahead a bit faster. That can be frustrating! I have learned not to get upset when I see drivers in the other lane move ahead of me. I have seen how those in the slower lane eventually catch up to drivers who raced ahead.

   This example can also help us not to despair when it feels like our plans are not moving quickly enough or in the direction we imagined. We do not know the wonder of God's plans or timing; it is in God's hands. What we can do is keep to our own pace and do our part in God's kingdom without worrying about those who move at a different pace. God will always be by our side.

Prayer: *Divine ruler of time and space, help us trust that at the appropriate time your plans and promises for us will be fulfilled. As Jesus taught us, we pray, 'Our Father which art in heaven, Hallowed be thy name. Thy kingdom come. Thy will be done, as in heaven, so in earth. Give us day by day our daily bread. And forgive us our sins; for we also forgive every one that is indebted to us. And lead us not into temptation; but deliver us from evil' (Luke 11:2–4, KJV). Amen.*

Thought for the day: 'For everything there is a season and a time for every matter under heaven' (Ecclesiastes 3:1).

Farlin Vanessa De Los Santos Mejía (Dominican Republic)

God chose me first

Read John 15:12–17

'You did not choose me, but I chose you. And I appointed you to go and bear fruit, fruit that will last, so that the Father will give you whatever you ask him in my name.'
John 15:16 (NRSV)

I was four years old when Mum's best friend invited us to Bible school. It was there that the Spirit of God touched my young heart. Since my parents didn't attend church, I wasn't able to go again until three years later when my family moved across town. Playing in the yard one day, I noticed the steeple on a church down the street. I had no memory of church, but I had the desire to go. One day I ran from the yard into the house and told my mum I needed her. When we got outside, I pointed to the steeple and blurted out, 'I want to go there!' She remained silent for a moment before giving me permission. When the day arrived, she watched intently as I made my way safely to Sunday school. From then on I attended church regularly.

At age 10, I invited Jesus into my heart. Afterwards, I began praying for my parents to attend church. I was in my mid 30s when Mum and Dad started going to worship. A few years later, my dad walked down the aisle and accepted Christ as his Saviour. Years passed, and at the age of 89, Mum asked Jesus into her heart.

As a young child, before I knew anything about God, God had chosen me. And in the proper timing, God answered my prayers.

Prayer: *Heavenly Father, before we were created, you knew us. You chose us before we chose you! Thank you for loving us enough to send your Son. Amen.*

Thought for the day: God always answers prayers.

Gaylen A. Carpenter (Tennessee, USA)

A sign

Read 1 Kings 19:11–18
*After the earthquake came a fire, but the Lord was not in the fire.
And after the fire came a gentle whisper.*
1 Kings 19:12 (NIV)

I once had an old bicycle with a broken pedal. I needed to go to a bike shop to find the right replacement. I knew there was a shop nearby, but I could not remember the name or location. After some research, I found a shop and made the trip there. The road to the bike shop was one that I travelled frequently. As I approached, I noticed a giant billboard advertising the shop with directions to 'turn here'. Shaking my head, I thought: *How many times have I passed that sign and never noticed it?* It was hard to miss.

After laughing at myself, I wondered how many times I have missed God's signs for me. I often pray for something and try to wait patiently for God's response. But perhaps God has already responded, and I'm just not focused on the right thing. I often look for an answer that makes sense to me, but God's response may be unexpected. In today's scripture reading, God wasn't in the earthquake or fire, God was in the whisper. We don't always know how God will answer us, but God will answer, even if it's how we least expect.

Prayer: *Dear God, may we approach you in prayer with confidence, understanding that you hear us and know our hearts. Give us the patience to wait faithfully for your response. Amen.*

Thought for the day: God's presence is all around me.

Brian Foster (North Carolina, USA)

A journey through grief

Read Psalm 147:1–3

He heals the broken-hearted and binds up their wounds.
Psalm 147:3 (NIV)

'Dear Lord,' I prayed, 'I feel as though I have reached the bottom of despair.'
I was on my way home from my son's funeral. What right did the people
on the streets have to be happy? Why was the musician allowed to play
a merry tune outside of the music store as I passed by? My world was
shattered. Didn't they understand?

The road loomed ahead of me out into the darkness. Then to my
astonishment, as I approached a small village, an illuminated cross on
a church came into my view. God, you are with me, I thought. You know
the depth of my sorrow. The cross reminded me of the suffering Jesus
endured for me, and I was comforted.

I knew that in time I would have to accept my son's sudden death.
Denial was not a choice. I began to realise I had been blessed to have had
my son in my life for 33 years. Time is indeed a healer, but this fact is of
no comfort when grief first strikes. As time has gone by, the lives of my
relatives and friends have returned to normal but mine has not. Working
through grief isn't easy, but it is necessary. And I know that only God's
constant love can deliver us from despair.

Prayer: *Dear Lord, thank you for being with us as we walk through the
valley of death. Amen.*

Thought for the day: Even in my deepest grief, God's healing love
will find me.

Sylvia Engen Espe (Alberta, Canada)

Freely given

Read Matthew 7:7–12

Here I am! I stand at the door and knock. If anyone hears my voice and opens the door, I will come in and eat with that person, and they with me.
Revelation 3:20 (NIV)

I headed to the front door after hearing an abrupt knock, hoping it hadn't woken my toddler. I wasn't happy about the prospect of telling yet another sales representative that I didn't want what they were offering. So imagine my surprise when I opened the door and instead saw three bouncy, smiling children! One exclaimed, 'We're selling cards!' and held up a few loose greeting cards. When I asked how much they cost, the little boy said, 'No, lady, it doesn't cost money. It's for free!' They handed me a card, then bounded off, leaving me happy but perplexed. This well-worn and discoloured greeting card made me smile, and the pleasant memory of these children knocking at my door has lasted many decades.

Frequently, I think I know who's knocking at the door. Too often, I expect that cost will be involved. Thankfully that's not God's way of giving. God comes to the door with gifts in hand, and they are given freely.

God uses the simplest of gifts to make a lasting impact on our lives. When we give to others and serve God, we can help God to bless others.

Prayer: *Lord Jesus, help us to receive with gratitude the gifts that come to us. May we be willing to take time from our schedules and open the doors you knock on today. Amen.*

Thought for the day: When God knocks, I will answer.

Nancy Nye Spasic (Texas, USA)

Surviving the storms

Read Isaiah 40:25–31

*He gives strength to the weary and increases the power
of the weak.*
Isaiah 40:29 (NIV)

It was an unseasonably warm late-winter afternoon, and I was working in the yard. I had planted three small white oak trees the previous year, but now they were bent over and sad looking. They had tried to withstand the gusty winter winds on their own, but they weren't strong enough. I hammered posts into the ground next to each tree and tied the trees to the posts, giving them the support they needed to stand up straight.

A few days later, I woke up to a significant storm. The temperature had dropped sharply, it was snowing and the wind was gusting up to 40 miles per hour. I walked to the window and looked out at my trees to see how they were withstanding the storm. Each tree, now supported by the sturdy posts, stood straight in the howling winds.

Like my small trees, we aren't equipped to stand on our own – especially when storms come. Thankfully, we have multiple 'posts' to help support us during difficult times. God's word, the Holy Spirit, and the love and care of our communities all help us endure. If we anchor ourselves to God, we can withstand the harshest storms.

Prayer: *Heavenly Father, thank you for supporting us when the storms of life threaten us. May we find courage and peace in you. Amen.*

Thought for the day: I will put my trust and faith in God, who carries me through hard times.

Clint Taylor (Illinois, USA)

Changing seasons

Read Ecclesiastes 3:1–8

I will rejoice in the Lord, I will joy in the God of my salvation.
Habakkuk 3:18 (KJV)

Just as the seasons change, we experience different seasons in our lives. My family is currently going through a difficult season. My four-year-old granddaughter has had an extensive bladder operation, and we are exhausted from time spent at her bedside in the hospital. But we are confident that God is merciful and will bring us through this season. There will come a time of rejoicing.

The prophet Habakkuk experienced a season where everything seemed to be going wrong. Still, he was determined to rejoice in God and have faith (see Habakkuk 3:17–19). In Habakkuk 3, the prophet proclaims his confidence in God.

Maybe you are going through a dreaded season right now – one that involves sickness, financial difficulties, broken relationships or grief – but these things will pass. In all circumstances, we can continually give thanks for God's mercy and grace.

Prayer: *Dear Lord, thank you for being with us through the changing seasons of our lives. Amen.*

Thought for the day: I will rejoice in God's presence with me today and always.

Valerie Clark (KwaZulu-Natal, South Africa)

God's surprises

Read Proverbs 16:1–9

I know the plans I have for you, says the Lord, plans for your welfare and not for harm, to give you a future with hope.
Jeremiah 29:11 (NRSV)

Every summer, I look forward to planting a vegetable garden. My planning begins in early spring when I carefully select my seeds and plot where they will be sown. However, things don't always grow as I anticipate. There are always plants that sprout and then wither before they can produce fruit. Often there are vegetables that flourish from seeds planted in the previous year or from seeds dropped by birds and other animals that share my yard. This year I reaped two large turnips which grew unexpectedly among my collard greens.

I've come to love these happy surprises. Often these rogue plants grow better and yield more at harvest time than the ones I've purposely planted and nurtured.

Throughout my life, I have carefully plotted and nurtured plans only to find that God has something else in store for me. After I was laid off from my long-term employment, a new career with more satisfying work emerged. After I was forced to leave the home I thought I would live in for the rest of my life, a more suitable home became available. When things don't work out the way we plan, we can hold on to hope in God's future for us and rejoice in God's surprises.

Prayer: *All-knowing God, help us to follow where you lead. Together we will rejoice in the destination. Amen.*

Thought for the day: Today I will rejoice in God's surprises.

Monica A. Andermann (New York, USA)

PRAYER FOCUS: TO CULTIVATE JOY IN SPITE OF DISAPPOINTMENTS

Unexpected help

Read Matthew 5:5–8
'Your Father knows what you need before you ask him.'
Matthew 5:8 (NIV)

I usually work from home, speaking to my colleagues through a set of earphones that I plug into my computer. They're not glamourous, but they work. One afternoon, I was over-reaching for a pen and the wire knocked over a glass of water that was on my desk. Quickly, I grabbed a towel and mopped most of it up; fortunately nothing was damaged.

Later, I began taking everything off my desk to make sure it was all completely dry. As I did so, I found a small conference speaker that I used to use instead of my earphones. I had thought that I'd lost it in the office some time ago, so to find it again was good news. But more than that, it was timely – I knew I would have an important interview four days later, where it would be better to use the conference speaker than my earphones.

I was reminded of how God knows what we need before we need it. I hadn't been worrying about using my earphones, but it seems God had other plans and made them known to me at the right time. It also gave me comfort that God is invested in my future.

Prayer: *Loving Father, thank you that you know what we need before we do and that your Spirit intercedes for us on our behalf. Help us to trust in your goodness when we experience disruption, and bring us joy as we see how you have anticipated our needs. Amen.*

Thought for the day: 'In all things, God works things for the good of those who love him' (Romans 8:28).

Christine Woolgar (England, United Kingdom)

God's transforming love

Read 1 Timothy 1:12–17
Here is a trustworthy saying that deserves full acceptance:
Christ Jesus came into the world to save sinners.
1 Timothy 1:15 (NIV)

In his early life, John Newton was involved in the brutal and inhumane business of capturing and selling African slaves. However, through a series of harrowing experiences, he began to question the moral implications of his actions. During a violent storm at sea, he cried out to God for mercy and his life was miraculously spared. This near-death encounter with the Divine sparked a deep spiritual awakening within him. But Newton's transformation didn't happen overnight. He spent years seeking God's grace and forgiveness, wrestling with guilt and shame for his past actions.

Eventually, he found solace in the words of the Bible, particularly in Paul's letter to Timothy. 'I was shown mercy so that in me, the worst of sinners, Christ Jesus might display his immense patience as an example for those who would believe in him and receive eternal life' (1 Timothy 1:16). Newton recognised that, even as the 'worst' sinner, he was not beyond the reach of God's love and redemption.

Everyone can experience God's love and forgiveness. Like Newton, we may have moments of doubt, guilt and shame, but through God's love, we can find healing and restoration.

Prayer: *Dear God, as we read the Bible, help us to apply its teachings to our lives. May it draw us closer to your boundless love and grace. Amen.*

Thought for the day: No one is beyond the reach of God's transforming love.

Dozie Ashiegbu (Abia, Nigeria)

God's jigsaw

Read 1 Corinthians 12:12–20

But in fact God has placed the parts in the body, every one of them, just as he wanted them to be.
1 Corinthians 12:18 (NIV)

I run a free jigsaw puzzle library and, at times, do some of the puzzles myself. It thrills me to see the completed picture, but sometimes there are a few pieces missing and I'm disappointed. I search through the pot of 'found pieces' and, if they're not there, will remove from circulation the incomplete jigsaws. Borrowers will tell me if the puzzle they are returning is short of pieces and occasionally that there is a piece that doesn't belong in the box.

God is good at puzzles. In his puzzles we are the pieces that he slots into place. He doesn't make mistakes like I do, each piece is exactly where it is meant to be and in the correct box. He doesn't lose pieces either. Each of his puzzles are complete and form a beautiful picture. Unfortunately we don't see the picture now – it won't be obvious until we get to heaven.

Throughout my life, I have struggled with the feeling that I don't belong. If I did something else, perhaps moved or changed job, I might belong. It's been hard to believe that I am where God wants me to be – until my last move. In my retirement, I've accepted his will and relaxed into the place he's put me, the place where I know I belong.

Prayer: *Dear God, encourage me to use my gifts in the place you have put me. Amen.*

Thought for the day: I will help others to understand that we are all where God wants us to be.

Lorna Clark (England, United Kingdom)

First Sunday of Advent

Read Luke 4:14–22

'The Spirit of the Lord is upon me, because he hath anointed me to preach the gospel to the poor; he hath sent me to heal the broken-hearted, to preach deliverance to the captives, and recovering of sight to the blind, to set at liberty them that are bruised.'
Luke 4:18 (KJV)

Sharing God's love with others, as Jesus did, should be our heart's desire. Our words and deeds can be a bright light for others and make a difference in this dark world. Our message of hope can heal the broken-hearted and bring cheer to the downcast.

One year, my friends and I made a plan to celebrate Christmas with people living in nursing homes. We prepared activities, small gifts and food to bring us all together. My heart was touched when I saw how happy the people were as we visited with them. The warmth of God's love filled us as we sang Christmas songs together. By showing them care, we provided comfort and lifted their spirits and ours as well.

This experience reminds me how meaningful it is to tell others the good news of Jesus' love, which can change our lives. As Christians, we have a commitment to follow Jesus and share the good news of the gospel. In doing so, we will find a special purpose for our lives as we share God's love with others.

Prayer: *Dear Jesus, thank you for the gift of your love. May we be your helping hands to reach those who are in need. Amen.*

Thought for the day: I will share God's love with those who feel burdened.

Kumalawaty Sundari (Jakarta, Indonesia)

Waiting for morning

Read Psalm 130

My soul waits for the Lord more than those who watch for the morning, more than those who watch for the morning.
Psalm 130:6 (NRSV)

I find the psalmist's words a challenge: my soul waits for the Lord, more than those who watch for the morning. Does it? Really?

When I was a junior doctor, I used to dread night shifts. In one hospital, nights meant a small team looking after multiple patients, right across the site. The long corridors, normally bustling by day, were dark, lonely and downright eerie by night. Towards the end of one particularly difficult shift, I remember the overwhelming relief of standing by a window, watching the sun rise. The emerging light meant the night was almost over. Morning was coming.

The watchman in the psalm also waits in the darkness for the first light of dawn. He doesn't doubt that morning will come but wonders when it will arrive. So too the psalmist. He writes from 'the depths' (v. 1), yet resolves to wait for the rescue God has promised.

Despite all the fairy lights and tinsel, Advent is about waiting for the return of the light in the darkest part of the year. Like the psalmist, we long for that dawn of redeeming grace, when sin and suffering will be abolished. Let's take time this season to celebrate the hope we have in the final, triumphant return of the light. The light shines in the darkness, and the darkness can never extinguish it (John 1:5).

Prayer: *Thank you, God, for the message of Advent. May we receive a fresh vision of the psalmist's hope this month. Amen.*

Thought for the day: Advent is about waiting for the return of the light.

Helen Hewitt (England, United Kingdom)

Stop and breathe

Read Psalm 85:8–13

'Peace I leave with you; my peace I give to you. I do not give to you as the world gives. Do not let your hearts be troubled, and do not let them be afraid.'
John 14:27 (NRSV)

A flat tyre? Not today! I had a critical appointment that morning, 90 miles away. I had only one hour to get the tyre fixed and still leave on time.

The only tyre shop in town was likely to be crowded, so I prayed for quick service. As I waited, my anxiety rose with every loud tick of the giant clock on the wall. Finally, I conceded, 'Lord, there's nothing I can do. It's in your hands. Please give me peace.' Waiting there, I heard this verse: 'Peace I leave with you; my peace I give to you.' Suddenly I understood what that meant. God has already given us peace. We don't have to keep asking for it, but we do have to take it in. So there in that shop that smelled of tyres and popcorn, I breathed in God's peace. My shoulders relaxed, and my anxiety lifted. With a few minutes to spare, my car was ready and I made it to my appointment.

Circumstances still threaten to overwhelm me at times, until I remember that verse. Then I stop, breathe in God's peace, and say to myself: 'Relax, God's got this.'

Prayer: *Lord Jesus, help us not to lose focus but to remember that you have already given us your peace. In every situation, help us to walk in your peace, trusting in your power to calm our hearts. Amen.*

Thought for the day: Each day I will breathe in God's peace.

Teresa Ambord (California, USA)

A servant's heart

Read John 13:1–17

*'If I, your Lord and teacher, have washed your feet, you too must wash
each other's feet.'*
John 13:14 (CEB)

My grandfather pastored a local congregation for 20 years. Through the
years, he became a father figure to them. When he died, this faith family,
along with our biological family, was deeply grieved.

As I was mourning and pouring my heart out to the Lord, looking
for comfort, God directed my affection and attention to my brothers
and sisters in this church. I felt led to comfort and serve them even as
I grieved. I was reminded of when Jesus poured water into a basin and
began to wash the disciples' feet, setting an example of servant leadership for them and for us.

As I reflected on this further, I began to understand the heart of this
teaching, although it isn't part of my culture to wash another person's
feet. Jesus calls us to seek ways to serve others, to be willing and ready
to respond to their needs. In my case, I felt called to be present with the
community, to be a listening ear, to mourn with them, and to give and
receive comfort in a difficult time. This is the way of life Jesus calls us
to – a life that reflects a servant's heart.

Prayer: *Dear God, help us seek ways to serve others and respond to
others' needs in obedience to Jesus' example. Amen.*

Thought for the day: I will follow Jesus' example by giving my time
and energy to serve others.

Quennie Joyce Ibarra (Misamis Occidental, Philippines)

Encourage one another

Read 1 Thessalonians 5:4–11

Encourage one another and build each other up,
just as in fact you are doing.
1 Thessalonians 5:11 (NIV)

After I retired, I worked part-time at a hardware store. But I was surprised when the boss didn't even talk to me! He never even gave me directions or assignments. Each day, I had to guess at what I was to do. I longed for some indication of how I was doing. I was hungry for encouragement, but it never came.

Finally, after several months, I asked him if he approved of my efforts. He laughed as if I should have known what he had been thinking. 'You're fantastic!' he said. 'You've cleaned up the place nicely. Even the regional manager has noticed. And every time the delivery truck comes, you get the product out on the shelves on time.' I swelled with pride and a sense of accomplishment. I had finally gotten encouragement, but it was sad that I had to wait so long.

As Christians, we need to encourage others. Many people are desperate for attention; they may feel lonely, neglected or unsuccessful. They may feel unloved and unwanted.

Why do we withhold our encouraging affirmation of others? It could be apathy, ignorance or simply a lack of love. Whatever the reason, let's break our habit of silence and pick up the habit of offering loving encouragement to others.

Prayer: *Dear God, help us to take advantage of opportunities to encourage others. Help us remember the gifts of encouragement we have received. Amen.*

Thought for the day: Our encouragement can change a person's life.

Clint Eastman (Massachusetts, USA)

'Peace be with you!'

Read John 20:19–23

On the evening of that first day of the week, when the disciples were together... Jesus came and stood among them and said, 'Peace be with you!'
John 20:19 (NIV)

Recently, a school shooting took place near my city. For days, headlines about the loss of lives and the hurting families saturated the news. Preoccupied with thoughts of the victims and their loved ones, as a chaplain I wanted to help. I earnestly prayed for those affected by the attack and then drove to the town to offer pastoral care to the hospital staff who treated the children. I listened with empathy to the nurses' heart-wrenching stories and prayed with them. I returned home in shock and disbelief.

My usual sense of well-being became unsteady; I felt vulnerable and fearful. Questions filled my mind, and sleep eluded me. As I lay waiting for sleep to come, I remembered another incident of violence: the crucifixion. In response, the confused and grieving disciples hid behind closed doors. Rocked by what they had witnessed, the future appeared full of unknowns. Then Jesus entered the locked room and stood among them, saying, 'Peace be with you.' The risen Son of God came, bringing reassurance in their turmoil and the gift of divine presence.

That restless night, I whispered the words of Jesus, 'Peace be with you.' A calm came over me. The moment became sacred in Christ's presence.

Prayer: *Come, Lord Jesus, enter our fearful places. Bring the peace and comfort of your presence. Amen.*

Thought for the day: In the midst of turmoil, God gives me the gift of divine presence.

Charleen Burghardt (Texas, USA)

The gift of love

Read Luke 2:1–7

While they were there, the time came for the baby to be born, and she gave birth to her firstborn, a son. She wrapped him in cloths and placed him in a manger, because there was no guest room available for them.

Luke 2:6–7 (NIV)

As the Christmas season drew near, my recent health issues were limiting my ability to enjoy my usual seasonal activities. However, I found comfort in Luke's narrative about the birth of Jesus, especially as I considered the innkeeper.

Nothing is written about the person who did not give Mary and Joseph a room. Regardless, much has been said about him, judging him harshly because he didn't give the expecting, travel-weary couple a room to stay in. Luke 2:7 says there simply wasn't a room to offer. But rather than turn Mary and Joseph away, the innkeeper offered them lodging in the stable. This action was creative and loving, an example of someone doing what he could with what was available to him. And when the angels appeared to the shepherds, they were told they would find the baby lying in a manger. This unusual detail likely helped them find Jesus.

So what can we do this Christmas season with what is available to us? Let us share the love God has shown us through our kindness, by listening to and helping others, and by praying with and for them. Seemingly insignificant actions can demonstrate God's love for us and others.

Prayer: *Dear God, help us to see the ways we can share your love with others. Remind us that our actions – no matter how big or small – demonstrate our love for you. Amen.*

Thought for the day: No act of love is small or insignificant to God.

Robert M. Terhune (Oregon, USA)

Second Sunday of Advent

Read Isaiah 61:1–7

*He has sent me to… provide for those who grieve in Zion –
to bestow on them a crown of beauty instead of ashes, the oil of joy
instead of mourning, and a garment of praise instead of a spirit
of despair.*
Isaiah 61:1, 3 (NIV)

A beloved Christmas tradition in the Dominican Republic is the exchange of gifts, called Angelitos (little angels). Names are written on pieces of paper that are placed in a container so people can randomly draw the name of the person to whom they will give a gift. Angelitos is a beautiful tradition shared within families, church communities and among colleagues. It fosters the generosity characteristic of the Christmas season.

In Isaiah 61, we read of God's promise to humankind – the brokenhearted, those in prison, those who mourn, the afflicted – that offers the good news of an exchange: 'A crown of beauty instead of ashes, the oil of joy instead of mourning and a garment of praise instead of a spirit of despair.' All this is available not only at Christmastime but all year round through faith in Jesus Christ. No wonder that when Jesus was born, the heavenly host appeared in Bethlehem, proclaiming peace and goodwill to all (see Luke 2:8–15).

I accepted Jesus as my Saviour in 2006, and this has been the best exchange of all – my former self for new life in Christ; my sins for God's forgiveness; my darkness for Christ's light.

Prayer: *God of good news, thank you for the gift of your Son
who offers us salvation. All glory be to you! Amen.*

Thought for the day: Christ's birth was the greatest gift of all.

Julianis Báez de Pichardo (Dominican Republic)

Courage to speak

Read Colossians 4:2–6

Faith comes from hearing the message, and the message is heard through the word about Christ.
Romans 10:17 (NIV)

Recently, while on holiday, I was talking with the young man who was setting out the beach chairs. During our conversation, I told him part of my faith story. He responded, 'What a coincidence; this is the second time today that someone has talked to me about God.' Then he told me that he was having a rough time and had moved here to get a fresh start – which led me to talk more about Jesus and the gospel. Eventually, I asked him if he felt that he wanted Jesus in his life. After he said yes, I called my wife over. The three of us prayed together, and he accepted Jesus right there on the beach.

God gives us opportunities like this one to witness. I also know I have missed opportunities or that I have seen them but did not have the courage to speak up. After all, even the apostle Paul, missionary that he was, asked for prayer to open doors and make his words clear when he spoke (see Colossians 4:2–4). I am thankful that God bolstered my courage in this instance and provided me with the words I needed.

Prayer: *Dear Lord, help us to share your love with others. Provide us with the words we need to say and the courage to say them. Amen.*

Thought for the day: When I have the courage to witness, God will give me the words to say.

Kim Koratsky (Tennessee, USA)

Three-way vision

Read Matthew 14:22–33

Peter got out of the boat, started walking on the water, and came towards Jesus. But when he noticed the strong wind, he became frightened, and, beginning to sink, he cried out, 'Lord, save me!'
Matthew 14:29–30 (NRSV)

A few months ago, I was laid off from my job of over eleven years. I've been laid off twice before, but this one hit me so hard I became physically ill. A couple of weeks later, *The Upper Room* devotional featured Matthew 14:22–33 as its reading. The writer reminded me that instead of looking down into the stormy waters, I needed to look up. From then on, whenever I was getting discouraged about my job search, I reminded myself to 'look up'.

Soon after, my pastor's Sunday sermon talked about looking up in trust, looking back in gratitude and looking forward in hope. I realised that in addition to looking up, I should look back and be thankful for the great jobs God has provided for me. Looking in both of these directions gives me the strength also to look forward in the hope that God will provide for me again.

Since then, I've encountered that same passage of Matthew in two subsequent issues of *The Upper Room*. These devotionals, along with the words from my pastor, have reinforced my resolve to continue to 'look up in trust, look back in gratitude and look forward in hope'.

Prayer: *Dear Jesus, thank you for reminding us to trust and follow the path you set for us. Amen.*

Thought for the day: God's loving provision gives me hope.

Peg Foltz (Illinois, USA)

Help my unbelief

Read Mark 9:14–29
The father of the child cried out, 'I believe; help my unbelief!'
Mark 9:24 (NRSV)

We were told by the doctor that our two-year-old daughter had severe anaemia and that we needed to take her to the hospital for further tests. I was frightened! Were we going to lose her? I tried to pray, but the whole time doubt and unbelief conquered my thoughts. The only prayer I was able to say was from Mark 9:24: 'Help my unbelief!'

I opened my Bible and read the whole story about the father and his child who was having seizures, and something occurred to me: the focus of this story was not the sick child but the despairing father! And Jesus met him with love and understanding. The child was healed in spite of his father's unbelief. This story made me feel at ease, and I put my child in God's loving hands. God took care of her, and today she is 52 years old and a mother to six wonderful children.

Prayer: *Dear Lord, your love has no limits. Thank you for your forgiving and healing grace. We pray in the name of Jesus who taught us to pray: 'Our Father which art in heaven, Hallowed be thy name. Thy kingdom come, Thy will be done in earth, as it is in heaven. Give us this day our daily bread. And forgive us our debts, as we forgive our debtors. And lead us not into temptation, but deliver us from evil: For thine is the kingdom, and the power, and the glory, for ever. Amen' (Matthew 6:9–13, KJV).*

Thought for the day: 'If we are faithless, he remains faithful – he cannot deny himself' (2 Timothy 2:13).

Øystein Brinch (Vestfold, Norway)

A new way of praying

Read James 4:6–10
Draw near to God, and he will draw near to you. Cleanse your hands, you sinners, and purify your hearts, you double-minded.
James 4:8 (NRSV)

I used to grumble to God about people and situations I didn't like. Despite being nice to the people who had wronged me, I remained bitter. I couldn't have an honest talk with God because my heart was filled with resentment. I finally realised that while I was kind to others face-to-face, I was meditating on their wrongs in my thoughts – and in my prayers. I wanted a pure heart.

I started to thank God for working in my worst situations. From my heart, I blessed the people who had harmed me and thanked God for them. With the help of the Holy Spirit, I obeyed God's command to forgive. Soon, I found I held nothing against anyone or any situation. My love for others became genuine. Then a miraculous thing happened: the room in my heart that had been filled with bitterness and grumbling was cleared out. As I prayed, I was no longer concerned with the sins of others or bitter about frustrating situations. My heart was free to draw near to God.

Prayer: *O God, show us if there is any sin, bitterness or complaining in our hearts so that we can repent of those things. We praise you for working in the worst situations of our lives, teaching us the power of forgiveness. Amen.*

Thought for the day: Today I will let God's love purify my heart.

Kaitlin Potts (Arizona, USA)

God is bigger

Read John 14:15–27

I will not leave you comfortless: I will come to you.
John 14:18 (KJV)

In the third month of my pregnancy, I was diagnosed with dengue, a urinary tract infection and typhoid fever. My doctor referred me to the hospital for better care. As I lay on my hospital bed, questions filled my mind: *Will my illnesses affect the growth and development of the foetus? Will I suffer a miscarriage?* When I began to experience mild bleeding, I started to lose hope. Stress and tension filled my heart and mind, and my eyes were filled with tears. But the words in Isaiah 41:10 gave me new strength and hope: 'Fear thou not; for I am with thee: be not dismayed; for I am thy God.'

I recovered and was discharged from the hospital after ten days. A week later, I went for my regular checkup and was relieved to learn that the baby was healthy, and its growth had not been affected by my health condition. To me, this was a miracle from God, and I rejoiced and gave thanks.

When we face insurmountable situations and challenges, we often feel helpless and alone. But God never abandons us. We can find strength knowing that God is bigger than any problem we face. Trusting this, we can have faith and keep moving forward with patience and a positive mindset.

Prayer: *Heavenly Father, we come before you with hearts full of gratitude. You are our refuge and strength. Thank you for the miracles you work in our lives and for your peace that surpasses all understanding. Amen.*

Thought for the day: No matter how big my problems are, God is bigger.

Liza Diarsa (Gujarat, India)

Little ones

Read Matthew 18:1–5

'Whoever welcomes one such child in my name welcomes me.'
Matthew 18:5 (NIV)

Once when I was out with colleagues, something they said that was intended lovingly instead made me feel small. I felt like the things I had been through and achieved had been belittled. This got to me, because like most people, I find myself longing to be respected by others.

When the disciples asked Jesus who in the kingdom of heaven was the greatest, I wonder what they thought his answer would be. Perhaps they wanted recognition for their loyalty and hard work. Jesus answers by calling over a little child to stand among them – that is, someone whose relationship with Jesus has nothing to do with work or accomplishment. Then Jesus tells them that unless they 'become like little children', they will not even be able to enter the kingdom of heaven, let alone be considered the greatest.

Longing to be respected by others is natural, but it can prevent us from recognising our inherent value, just as we are, as people created and loved by God. If we think that our worth is in what we have accomplished or the positions of honour we find ourselves in, we lose the essence and joy of God's kingdom. What's more, we may start to look at others that way, too. The truth is that we are all welcome in God's kingdom as his beloved children.

Prayer: *Father God, help us to recognise that our true value comes from being made and loved by you, not anything we do. Amen.*

Thought for the day: 'See what great love the Father has lavished on us, that we should be called children of God! And that is what we are!' (1 John 3:3).

Amy Turner (England, United Kingdom)

Third Sunday of Advent

Read Isaiah 35

The angel said to them, 'Do not be afraid, for see, I am bringing you good news of great joy for all the people.'
Luke 2:10 (NRSV)

During the four Sundays before Christmas, my church lights one candle each week on an Advent wreath to anticipate the birth of Jesus. Each candle represents an aspect of Christ's light coming into the world. On the third Sunday, we light the candle representing 'joy', which has special meaning for me.

Before I turned my life over to Christ, I was a sad person. But when I let God's Holy Spirit fill my heart, the first thing I experienced was great joy that bubbled up and flowed through me like fresh, sparkling water. This fountain of living water (see John 7:37–39) lightened my burdens and healed the hurts that had made me sad.

Since then, I've had times of grief, disappointment and pain. Occasionally, I experience a dullness or disconnection in my personal relationships and while praying or reading scripture. But when I remember to focus on Jesus and other people instead of myself, the joyous living water flows again and revives me.

Sharing the good news of Jesus through words and actions allows God's living water to flow through us and spread to others. By being a channel for God's love, we can bring God's joy into the lives of others and increase the joy in ours.

Prayer: *Dear God, help us never to tire of sharing your blessings with others so that we may uplift them as you uplift us. Amen.*

Thought for the day: Jesus is my joy.

Mary Neumann (Georgia, USA)

Faithful response

Read Judges 6:11–27

The angel of the Lord appeared to him and said to him,
'The Lord is with you, you mighty warrior.'
Judges 6:12 (NRSV)

I love Bible stories like Gideon's, where someone suddenly finds themselves facing an enormous task that they don't feel qualified for. Gideon's initial response isn't exactly faith-filled, but the angel of the Lord tells him he is a mighty warrior. Over the course of several encounters with the angel, Gideon's faith grows to the point where he believes that God is going to help him do what God is asking, and he becomes that mighty warrior.

I can remember a time in my life when I felt God was calling me to leave the profession I was in and start on a new path of self-employment. There would be no regular hours and no guaranteed income. I would be learning how to get the business up and running with very limited experience, all at the age of 42. It was daunting but exciting! I trusted in God, and my family and I were blessed by my new work, as were my customers. Gideon also trusted God, and he and his family, along with all Israel, were blessed.

Prayer: *Trustworthy God, help us to hear your voice when you call. Help us be obedient to you even when we feel unprepared to do what you are asking of us. And help us know that you are always with us. Amen.*

Thought for the day: I can bless others by answering God's call.

Lee Watson (England, United Kingdom)

Simple wonders

Read Genesis 1:25–31

You who are the Lord's holy ones, honour him, because those who honour him don't lack a thing.
Psalm 34:9 (CEB)

Most mornings I walk our dog, Emma, along a country road near our home. Usually, we see some wildlife on our walks – deer, squirrels and rabbits. These sightings have become so routine that Emma knows where the deer tend to be and anticipates them by tugging on her leash and whining with excitement. Sometimes we come across a herd of does and fawns, occasionally with a young buck. Without Emma alerting me, I'm not sure I would notice the deer camouflaged in the woods.

This makes me pause and ask myself, *How many other blessings do I miss in the busyness of the day?* Often I have a list of tasks to get through. I check the tasks off one by one, showing how productive I can be and measuring my worth by what I get done. I try to resist the need to be productive at all times and simply enjoy the gifts of God's beautiful world when I see them. Stopping to savour the wonder of a herd of deer in the woods can be an act of worship.

God does not judge me by what I accomplish in a day. I can take the time to breathe in God's presence and enjoy the beautiful creation around me as I worship and praise God, my creator.

Prayer: *Dear Lord, thank you for your hidden treasures. Help us to take the time to search them out and praise you when we find them. Amen.*

Thought for the day: Today I will pause to notice God's blessings around me.

Kathy Espenshade (Pennsylvania, USA)

Untimely grief

Read John 14:1–6

'My Father's house has many rooms; if that were not so, would I have told you that I am going there to prepare a place for you?'
John 14:2 (NIV)

At Christmas, a time full of great expectations of joy, death is an unwelcome visitor. Unfortunately, we have no guarantees that death will bypass the holiday season and choose some other, more 'convenient' time.

About three weeks before last Christmas, my only sister died. I was far away at the time and unable to visit her before her death. The previous year, a dear cousin and an aunt had died. So Christmas this year was bittersweet for me as I made plans to return home for my sister's memorial service.

As I thought of those I have lost these past few years, my parents among them, the words of John 14:2 came to me. I then pictured a banquet table set in one of those rooms with my parents, aunts and uncles, a cousin and my sister – gathered together for a heavenly meal. And at the centre of the table sat our Lord. The words of a Christmas hymn came to me: 'Emmanuel, God with us'. At Christmas, even in the depths of grief and loss, God promises to be with us as we celebrate our Saviour's birth.

Prayer: *God of peace, comfort all those experiencing grief this Christmas season. In the name of the one who conquered death and invites us to the heavenly table. Amen.*

Thought for the day: Christmas reminds us of Immanuel – God with us.

Mike Bertoglio (Washington, USA)

Don't forget to ask

Read Philippians 4:4–7

Do not be anxious about anything, but in every situation, by prayer and petition, with thanksgiving, present your requests to God.
Philippians 4:6 (NIV)

The Bible study I was leading didn't go well. People were distracted, and their comments were scattered. I couldn't seem to bring their attention back to the study. As I drove home after the meeting, I felt discouraged. Why had things gone wrong? Then I heard the Spirit's quiet voice: 'Did you ask me to help you?' I had not. In my frustration I hadn't thought to ask for God's help in refocusing our attention. I hadn't even asked God to guide me as I prepared the study.

Sometimes we don't receive from God because we don't ask. As I thought about how I could talk to God about my needs more consistently, I remembered Philippians 4:6 – 'Bring up all of your requests to God in your prayers and petitions' (CEB). I needed to ask God for wisdom in planning and making decisions, both in my morning quiet times and throughout the day.

We can cling to God's assurance: 'I will instruct you and teach you in the way you should go; I will counsel you with my loving eye on you' (Psalm 32:8). When we talk to God about our everyday needs, God will guide us.

Prayer: *God of love, thank you for your presence. Remind us to talk to you often and ask for your wisdom. In Jesus' name we pray. Amen.*

Thought for the day: I will make my needs and concerns known to God through prayer.

Sandi Somers (Alberta, Canada)

Spiritual stonework

Read Matthew 16:13–20

'I tell you that you are Peter, and on this rock I will build my church, and the gates of Hades will not overcome it.'
Matthew 16:18 (NIV)

Having grown up in an area known for its abundance of stone, I am fascinated by stonework. Travelling throughout the region, one can see houses, churches, walls and fences made of stone. While these structures age and are often covered with moss, they remain standing. I often think about the stonemasons who build these structures, admiring their craft of selecting imperfect stones, hewing them and placing them into structures that can stand the test of time.

Like a stonemason selecting, hewing and placing stones, Jesus did the same with his followers. In today's scripture reading, Jesus stated that Peter would be the rock on which he would build his church. Why Peter? After all, he would go on to deny Jesus three times on the night of his arrest (see Luke 22:54–62). However, scripture teaches us how Jesus uses all types of imperfect people to build his church. As he did with Peter, the Lord found a place for Paul, the former persecutor of Christians (see Acts 8:1–3). Although these people were flawed, Jesus still selected, hewed and placed them in the spiritual stonework that continues to stand the test of time.

Prayer: *Dear God, thank you for looking past our flaws and fitting us into your kingdom. Amen.*

Thought for the day: Although flawed, I can still be used in Christ's church.

Walter Battle (Tennessee, USA)

The greatest gift

Read Luke 2:15–20

They spread the word concerning what had been told them about this child, and all who heard it were amazed at what the shepherds said to them. But Mary treasured up all these things and pondered them in her heart.

Luke 2:17–19 (NIV)

When I was a child, I would stare up into the sky on Christmas night and wonder if the brightest star I could find was the same one that led the wise men to Jesus (see Matthew 2:1–12). The thought of the miracle born to us would fill my heart with happiness and awe.

Years later I was expecting my first son, who was also due to be born in December. After trying for almost five years to have a baby, I was filled with expectation and excitement. I had a new appreciation for Mary waiting for the arrival of the newborn king. My son was born the week before Christmas, and that was the most special Christmas I had ever experienced. I marvelled at the miracle of life.

Luke 2:19 tells us that after the shepherds visited Mary, she 'treasured up all these things and pondered them in her heart'. What wonder and awe must have filled her!

I never want to forget the glory of the Word made flesh or the powerful love God has for each of us. The greatest gift has already been given. We need only to receive it and do our best to lead others to this gift as well.

Prayer: *Loving God, thank you for the gift of a restored relationship with you, given through Jesus. May our relationship with you continually grow and fill us with hope and wonder each day. Amen.*

Thought for the day: God's love is more beautiful than I can imagine.

Kelly Hays (Michigan, USA)

Fourth Sunday of Advent

Read Psalm 42:5–8

I say to God my Rock, 'Why have you forgotten me? Why must I go about mourning?'
Psalm 42:9 (NIV)

It was the week before Christmas, and I was pouting. 'Bah, humbug, God; I'm estranged from my family so I'll sit here alone again and make my own dinner. At least I hope you'll be with me.'

Then, on Thursday my friend Wally took me to the senior centre for a wonderful Christmas dinner. On Sunday, friends George and Jan took me to our church Christmas service. Then I went out to lunch with several friends, and George and Jan took me back to the evening carol service. It was a beautiful day! On Christmas afternoon, my friend Larry brought me a wonderful Christmas dinner. Later that day Wally sent me another feast that he cooked himself. I also received several calls, texts and emails wishing me a Merry Christmas.

At the end of a wonderful day, I thought, God even listens to us when we are whining! 'Forgive me, Lord,' I prayed, 'for allowing my mind to forget the magnificent gift you gave us at Christmas.'

God's love blesses us beyond our ability to understand, sending others to sustain us when we feel lost and alone. Wrapped in the arms of God, we are never forgotten.

Prayer: *Listening God, forgive us when we forget your powerful love. When we wander and forget your loving presence, stay with us. Amen.*

Thought for the day: Even when I move away from God, God moves closer to me.

Ken Claar (Idaho, USA)

PRAYER FOCUS: THOSE FEELING FORGOTTEN   121

Final words

Read Matthew 28:18–20

My mouth is filled with your praise, declaring your splendour all day long.
Psalm 71:8 (NIV)

Sometimes I ask myself, *What will be the last words people hear from me?* The last words I heard from my cousin Javier were: 'Take care of yourself, dear.' He died from a heart attack the following day. I remember, too, a friend who lived in another city and who loved God greatly. She would always end our phone conversations with 'God bless you.' These words from my cousin and friend encouraged me and showed their care for me.

I recall Jesus' final words to his disciples: 'You will receive power when the Holy Spirit comes on you; and you will be my witnesses in Jerusalem, and in all Judea and Samaria, and to the ends of the earth' (Acts 1:8). He calls them and all of us who follow him to proclaim his name, giving us the power to do so through the Holy Spirit.

Will my last words encourage or cause distress? Will they comfort or cause pain? We do not know what our final words will be, but if our words are filled with praise to God, surely those words will build up, encourage and bless those around us.

Prayer: *Source of all good things, help us to honour you and bless others with the words we speak. Amen.*

Thought for the day: 'Let the words of my mouth… be acceptable to you, O Lord' (Psalm 19:14, NRSV).

Estela Castellanos Díaz (Mexico City, Mexico)

Promise of light

Read John 1:1–14

'I am the light of the world: he that followeth me shall not walk in darkness, but shall have the light of life.'
John 8:12 (KJV)

After nearly 100 years, the beautiful stained-glass windows in our church needed repair. Plywood panels temporarily fill the empty spaces, and our sanctuary is much dimmer now. We're not sure how long the repairs will take, but we look forward to once again seeing the glorious hues of the windows in our sanctuary.

Sometimes I allow my own outlook to become dimmed by the condition of the world. It's disturbing and almost overwhelming – the wars, injustice, poverty, crime, prejudice and religious and political strife. So many problems seem to darken the world; many seem to have no solutions.

However, just as I know the sun will once again shine brilliantly through our stained-glass windows, scripture assures me of the promise that one day all will be revealed. The apostle Paul wrote in 1 Corinthians 13:12 that we are seeing things 'through a glass, darkly' but that one day all will become clear. Through faith and hope we anxiously anticipate the fulfilment of God's promise that one day we will understand and live in God's holy light.

Prayer: *Dear God, we thank you for the assurances you give us in your holy word that help us when we feel overwhelmed by the world. Amen.*

Thought for the day: When the world seems dark, I will look to Jesus, the light of the world.

Steven Schlesselman (Oklahoma, USA)

Christmas Eve

Read Matthew 11:27–30

'Glory to God in the highest heaven, and on earth peace to those on whom his favour rests.'
Luke 2:14 (NIV)

As evening approached, my spirit and eyelids drooped as the hurry and blur of holiday preparations took their toll. I had been joyfully anticipating the Christmas Eve candlelight service at my church. However, the darkness of the shorter winter day and a bone-chilling cold snap made me want to stay at home under a blanket. Although I was fading fast, I decided to leave early for church before I lost my motivation.

Once at church, I helped set out food for the hospitality hour. I wondered if attendance would be low due to the cold and the pull of holiday duties. I sat down in the front row of the empty church, feeling satisfied that I had managed to make it to the evening service despite my tiredness.

Wonder and joy overtook me as the first hymn resounded with booming, exuberant praise for our Saviour! I turned around and saw pews overflowing with people – families, visitors and friends. My flagging spirit was uplifted at the sight and sound! All of us were gathered to celebrate the mystery of the Christ child. As we joined in praise, celebration and fellowship, our Lord and Saviour refreshed our spirits.

Prayer: *Humble and gentle Saviour, refresh us with your loving presence, especially when life's responsibilities overwhelm us. Amen.*

Thought for the day: When I am weak, the Lord is strong.

Clare Kirkwood (New York, USA)

Christmas Day

Read Luke 2:8–14

'Your saviour is born today in David's city. He is Christ the Lord.'
Luke 2:11 (CEB)

My two young grandchildren arrived three days before Christmas to celebrate the holiday at my house. In the dining room, I had set out a decades-old nativity scene, except I left the manger empty. Baby Jesus' absence greatly concerned my four-year-old granddaughter. Straight away, she asked, 'Where's the baby?' I told her he would arrive Christmas morning, but she was not consoled.

Several times over the next three days she walked by the manger and commented, 'There's no baby.' Eventually, she took the matter into her own hands and placed the tiniest figure from my nesting doll in the crib. I told her that was not the baby Jesus and she replied, 'I know that', and merrily went on her way. On Christmas Eve, after my granddaughter went to sleep, I switched the nesting doll with the baby Jesus.

I was sipping coffee at the kitchen table early Christmas morning when I heard my granddaughter shout over and over, 'He is here! Baby Jesus is here!' She ran through the house to wake her family to the 'good news of great joy'. She paid no attention to her overflowing stocking or gifts from Santa. Her exuberant reaction helped me experience anew the good news of the arrival of the Christ child. Indeed, he is here! Baby Jesus is here!

Prayer: *Dear Lord God, may our hearts overflow with joy and praise this Christmas morning as we celebrate the gift of Christ Jesus. Amen.*

Thought for the day: Today and every day I can experience anew the joy of finding Jesus.

Nell Noonan (Mississippi, USA)

God's glimmers

Read 1 Thessalonians 5:12–24

Rejoice always, pray continually, give thanks in all circumstances;
for this is God's will for you in Christ Jesus.
1 Thessalonians 5:16–18 (NIV)

I recently learned about 'glimmers' – small moments in the day that make us feel joy, peace and gratitude. The more we train our brains to be on the lookout for these kinds of moments, the more they seem to happen.

Today's quoted scripture sounds to me a lot like looking for glimmers: always be joyful; never stop praying; be thankful in all circumstances.

For me, Christmas is like one continuous glimmer-full season, and I love it. In addition to the decor, food, gatherings and gifts, Christmas is a time when I see people smiling more and speaking more openly about Jesus.

As Christians, we are encouraged to share the gospel with others, and Christmas is the perfect time to do so. But we can also show the people around us how Jesus is at work in our lives all year long. Sharing the gospel can be a glimmer-full experience. Jesus is our peace and joy, and the more we speak about and share his goodness, the more we notice it around us.

Prayer: *Father God, thank you for your goodness. Help us to notice the glimmers of you in our daily lives. In Jesus' name. Amen.*

Thought for the day: Gratitude helps me to notice God at work in my life.

Danelle Pinnock (Jamaica)

Praise the Lord

Read Psalm 150

Let everything that has breath praise the Lord. Praise the Lord.
Psalm 150:6 (NIV)

When I was in secondary school, I played the trumpet. I can vividly remember trying to learn how to play. It took a lot of air! When I look back on this period, I give thanks because I was literally making 'a joyful noise' with the trumpet.

Of course there were times I did not want to play the trumpet. Sometimes I have days when I don't want to do anything. But what if I remembered that in everything I do, I can praise God? This is what I love about Psalm 150. It is a reminder to praise God continually for giving us breath for another day.

Now my son is learning to play the trumpet and my daughter is learning the flute. Every now and then I smile when I hear them practising. Their music is a gift, even when it's not played perfectly.

This is also true for life. We do not need to have everything in perfect order before we praise God. All we need to do is offer the very best we can in that moment. Praise and thanks be to God that we have been given breath!

Prayer: *Giver of Life, continue to breathe your life into us so we can live joyfully and praise you always. Amen.*

Thought for the day: I have breath, praise God!

Ryan Stratton (Texas, USA)

PRAYER FOCUS: MUSICIANS

The seeds we sow

Read Matthew 13:1–9

The seed falling on good soil refers to someone who hears the word and understands it. This is the one who produces a crop, yielding a hundred, sixty or thirty times what was sown.
Matthew 13:23 (NIV)

One Sunday, the lay youth leader at church had the children act out a scene from an old TV show. The moral of the lesson was that each of us has a mission from God to fulfil in our daily lives. I still think about that lesson every day. Since then, it has been my custom to ask God, 'What is my mission today?' Then I write down my daily to-do list, which usually includes humdrum tasks and chores. But occasionally I am inspired to add something else – send a note to a friend, call someone unable to leave home or do a task that takes me out of my comfort zone.

One day I mentioned to the youth leader how much that lesson had meant to me, and she replied, 'I don't remember that at all.' How curious, I thought. However, I have found that we often sow seeds of kind words or good deeds that we forget. They may go unappreciated, but sometimes they land where they do good. So I vowed to keep writing that list and checking it off in hopes that some God-inspired actions or words will fall on good soil, exactly where they need to be.

Prayer: *Dear God, open our hearts to your will, and help us to reach out to others with kind words and deeds. Thank you for surprising us with the joy of seeing our seeds of kindness take root.*
In Jesus' name, we pray. Amen.

Thought for the day: With God's help, my seeds of kindness can make a difference.

Rhea Sherburne Nyquist (Minnesota, USA)

Feeling lost

Read Psalm 139:1–10

If I rise on the wings of the dawn, if I settle on the far side of the sea, even there your hand will guide me, your right hand will hold me fast.
Psalm 139:9–10 (NIV)

It can be a terrifying feeling to lose your bearings and come to the realisation that you are lost. As a young teen at scout camp, the leaders would remind us that if we lost our way in the dark, we should walk towards the light of the campfire.

Getting lost can happen to anyone – not just physically, but mentally, emotionally and spiritually. In such circumstances, it is wonderful to have someone to lean on, a friend that comes alongside us, a guide to help us negotiate the unfamiliar terrain we are passing through.

Psalm 46:1 tells us that 'God is our refuge and strength, an ever-present help in trouble'. God will not abandon us. God knows where we are, what we need, and how to help us in our distress. When we are overwhelmed and feeling lost, we can look to Jesus, the light of the world, and ask for God's guidance.

Prayer: *Dear Lord, may we be ever mindful that you love us and will never forsake us. You are always near, even in our darkest hour. Please strengthen our faith and lift us up as we pray the prayer Jesus taught us: 'Our Father in heaven, hallowed be your name, your kingdom come, your will be done, on earth as it is in heaven. Give us today our daily bread. And forgive us our debts, as we also have forgiven our debtors. And lead us not into temptation, but deliver us from the evil one' (Matthew 6:9–13, NIV). Amen.*

Thought for the day: No matter my circumstances, God is always near.

Thomas Davis (Ontario, Canada)

The solid rock

Read Matthew 7:24–29

'The rain came down, the streams rose, and the winds blew and beat against that house; yet it did not fall, because it had its foundation on the rock.'
Matthew 7:25 (NIV)

For years, my parents owned a small cottage on the coast. It was a wonderful retreat and the perfect place to spend summers. But one particularly rough winter, an extreme storm surge wreaked havoc on our little house.

The storm was so severe that the water surge, torrential rain and monstrous waves began to erode the sand and rocks that surrounded the house. When the storm was over, we could see how the water had severely pulled away the soil in front of the house, exposing the foundation.

In spite of the storm's ferocity, however, the house was saved. Regardless of the beating it took, it stayed strong and standing. As I looked at the beach house, all I could think about was the parable that Jesus taught about the house built on a strong foundation. The scene in front of me was exactly what Jesus described. With its rock foundation, it would remain standing.

Just as our beach house remained standing because of its stone foundation, we can stand strong when our foundation is built on the truth of God, our Rock and our Redeemer.

Prayer: *Dear God, thank you for teaching us to keep your word in our hearts. It safeguards us against storms, shores up our foundation in you, and keeps us standing strong in your love. Amen.*

Thought for the day: Building my life on a foundation of faith creates a safe haven.

Heather Spiva (California, USA)

Helping your neighbours

Read 1 John 3:16–24

If someone has material possessions and sees a brother or sister in need but refuses to help – how can the love of God dwell in a person like that?
1 John 3:17 (CEB)

I had just brought my wife home from a cancer operation when a snow-storm hit. I'm in my late 80s and have a bad back, so shovelling the driveway was pressing on my mind. What if my wife had an emergency? Then I heard a noise and saw a neighbour girl clearing our driveway. Shortly after she arrived, a man across the street finished his driveway and came over to help her. I thanked them both, grateful to have such caring neighbours.

We got more snow, so by the next day we were snowed in again. The same girl returned, and this time another neighbour and his wife also shovelled the large drifts. When I opened the door to thank them, the girl said: 'Go back inside where it's warm – we'll finish this.'

I'm going to repay my neighbours in some way – perhaps I'll mow their yards next summer, give them gift certificates or take them baked goods. But I've already asked the Lord to be with them and provide them with helpers when they are in need.

Sometimes troubles bring unforeseen blessings from people we may have taken for granted. Let us thank God for those who help us!

Prayer: *Dear Lord, open our eyes to see what the people around us need. Show us then how to act in love, remembering what you have done for us. Amen.*

Thought for the day: Which of my neighbours can I help today?

Verl Lekwa (Iowa, USA)

Small group questions

3 September

1 What natural material reminds you of the importance of being tightly connected with others and working together? What examples from the natural world remind you of the problems caused by weak connections?

2 When has an experience brought your congregation closer together? What happened? What lasting changes have you observed from this experience?

3 Why do you think it is important to have unity and connection with other believers? Why is it so easy for disruption to impact a congregation?

4 What shared goals does your church currently have? How do these goals encourage church members to work together? How do they strengthen your congregation?

5 When have you participated in an outreach ministry? What did you do? How did this outreach connect you to others and to God?

10 September

1 When have you realised that someone you have known for a while is a Christian? How did you realise this? What happened when you learned they shared your faith?

2 How did you learn about God? How did learning about God change your life?

3 Recall an unexpected blessing you have received. What was it? How did this blessing impact you? How did it bring you closer to God and others?

4 Do you regularly speak about your faith with others? Why or why not? What happens when you speak about your faith openly?

5 How are you blessed and encouraged when you spend time connecting with other believers? Why do you think spending time with other Christians is so meaningful?

17 September

1 Who in your community is an example of giving generously out of what they have? Why? How does their example inspire you?

2 What limitations do you currently have? In what ways do you give to others despite those limitations?

3 Have you ever let adversity keep you from serving others and sharing what you have? Why or why not? What motivates you to keep giving to others regardless of the challenges?

4 When have you been blessed by someone who gave what they had? How did this blessing affect you? How did you show your appreciation?

5 Who in scripture serves as an example of giving to others no matter what challenges or limitations they had? What can you learn from their story?

24 September

1 Have you travelled alone? If so, what was it like? How do you think travelling alone differs from travelling with companions?

2 When have you decided to challenge yourself and leave your comfort zone? What happened?

3 Describe a time when you received an answer to your concerns before expressing them in prayer. How did you feel? How did this affect your relationship with God?

4 When has a message helped you feel better about your situation? Why was this message so meaningful for you? How did it remind you that God knows and cares for you?

5 What scripture verses remind you of God's presence? How do these verses help you when you are feeling worried or doubtful?

1 October

1 When have you or someone you know gone on a journey and had to bring everything needed to survive? What was the journey? How did relying on others become newly important during that time?

2 Recall a time when you witnessed a small gift making a huge difference. What was the gift? Why did it make such a difference?

3 Where in your life do you see strangers forming a community? In what ways does that community support its members? How have the strangers become 'neighbours'?

4 What small kindnesses do you offer to those around you? How do these encounters enrich your life? In what ways do you stay prepared and open to help those in need?

5 Consider your neighbours. Who needs help right now? How can you care for them? What small actions could make a big difference for them?

8 October

1 When have you witnessed seeds being scattered haphazardly? Were they tended to? Did any of them grow into plants?

2 Do you find it easy or difficult to share God's word with others? Why? What encourages you to share your faith even when it feels challenging?

3 When have you seen surprising results from talking about God? How does that situation inspire you to remain open to others who want to hear about God?

4 How do you provide continuing care and encouragement to the people you minister to? Why is it so important to be attentive to these connections?

5 What scripture verses encourage you to share your faith? What spiritual practices give you courage to share God's word?

15 October

1 When have you been worried about your health and safety? What did you do? How did your faith help you through that experience?

2 Recall a time when you came across a scripture verse that provided exactly what you needed. How did the verse help you? In what ways did you keep the verse close during that time?

3 Why do you think scripture has such power to help us overcome fear? What verses do you turn to when you are afraid? What prayers help allay your fears?

4 Who or what in your life helps you hold on to strength and hope? Why? How does this reminder help you trust God when you face challenges?

5 When has God been with you in moments of struggle and brokenness? Did you find it hard to notice God's presence in those moments? Why or why not? What helps you turn to God even when you feel broken?

22 October

1 When have you cared for someone in your community? How did the experience enrich your life and faith?

2 Recall a time when someone made the effort to check on you. Did you know the person? How did it feel to be cared for in this way?

3 When have you felt that you knew a stranger because of the way they reflect God's love and care? Why do you think someone's Christlike actions can make us feel closer to them?

4   What scripture verses help you remain open to the needs of others? What verses remind you of how important it is to care for others?

5   Who in your community needs a helping hand today? How can you care for them? What do you need today? How will you accept help from others?

29 October

1   When have you found that anticipation deepens your grief? Why do you think this happens? How do you avoid focusing on future pain?

2   How does God help you through painful times? How does prayer strengthen you when you're in pain? How does your faith help you remain hopeful in such times?

3   Do you find it easy to trust that God has a plan? Why or why not? How do you lean on God even when you don't know what the future holds?

4   Recall a painful time in your life. Who in scripture do you most relate to when you think about this time? How does their story encourage you and deepen your trust in God?

5   What prayers and spiritual practices comfort you in times of grief and uncertainty? How do you remain connected to God and keep trusting even when you are struggling?

5 November

1   Where do you lack confidence in your abilities? Why? How do you push yourself to get out of your comfort zone?

2   When have you experienced a barrier while trying to minister to someone? What was the barrier? What was the outcome of your efforts?

3   Describe a time when you felt the Holy Spirit at work in spite of your feelings of insufficiency. How do you know the Spirit was at work in that situation?

4 How do you relate to Moses in the story of the burning bush?
   Who else in scripture do you relate to when God leads you to do
   something you aren't sure you can do?

5 How does your church encourage you to remain open and willing to
   serve God in whatever way God calls you? How will you encourage
   others to accept God's call?

12 November

1 When have you felt surrounded by grief? How did this experience
   change the way you deal with grief?

2 Why do you think grief can teach us so much? What is the most
   meaningful lesson grief has taught you about God? What has it
   taught you about yourself and others?

3 Today's writer says there are depths of sorrow no human comfort
   can reach. Is there any sorrow God's comfort cannot reach?
   How do you commune with God when you are experiencing
   profound sorrow?

4 What does it mean to you that you cannot store up God's grace for
   tomorrow? Do you find it encouraging or discouraging that you
   cannot store up grace for future needs? Why?

5 What scripture passages remind you of God's comfort and grace
   in times of grief? How do you use these verses when you are
   experiencing painful situations?

19 November

1 When have you tried to get ahead in life only to realise your efforts
   were in vain? What did this teach you about trying to get ahead?

2 Why do you think it often seems that others are moving ahead
   faster than we are? How do you feel when you see others seeming
   to move faster than you? How do you trust God's timing in
   these moments?

3 Recall a time when your plans did not move ahead as quickly or in the direction that you had hoped. What happened? How did you respond?

4 What spiritual practices and scripture passages help you to work at your own pace? How do you avoid worrying about what others are doing and focus on your calling from God?

5 Who in your life serves as an example of following God's path without worrying whether others are going faster? How does their example inspire you to move forward in a similar way?

26 November

1 When have you observed a plant or something else in nature growing in an unexpected way? What did this teach you about the natural world? What did it teach you about God?

2 Do you enjoy the happy surprises nature provides? Why or why not? What is your favorite surprise from nature?

3 When have you carefully planned something that didn't work out? What did God have in store for you instead? Did you have an easy or hard time embracing God's plan?

4 Do you generally like surprises or not? Why? Do you feel differently about surprises from God? What helps you rejoice in the surprises God gives you?

5 Who in scripture cultivated joy despite facing disappointments? How did they do so? What can you learn from their story?

3 December

1 Who in your life has stepped into a parental role for you? How did their influence change you?

2 When have you poured out your heart to God looking for comfort? How did that connect you with God? In what ways did God offer you direction and comfort in that moment?

3   Have you ever felt led to comfort others even while you were in pain? If so, what did you do? If not, how do you think it would feel to comfort someone else despite your own grief?

4   How does the story of Jesus washing the disciples' feet encourage you to serve others? What other stories from Jesus' life encourage you to serve?

5   What are some ways you can comfort and help those who are grieving in your community today? How could you show them Jesus' love and comforting presence?

10 December

1   When have you or a loved one faced a scary medical issue? What did you think and feel while it was happening? What questions and worries came up for you?

2   Do doubts and fears make it hard for you to pray? If not, what other obstacles make prayer difficult for you? What do you do when you struggle to pray?

3   When you are experiencing difficult or scary times, how does scripture help you? What verses and stories do you find the most compelling in these times?

4   Have you ever struggled with unbelief? If so, what happened? How can you help someone struggling with unbelief today?

5   Recall a time when you read a scripture story and gained a new understanding of the story. Why do you think you gained this new perspective? How did this new understanding of the story help you?

17 December

1   Have you ever experienced loss during the Christmas season? If so, how did that loss affect your celebrations and feelings about the holiday? If not, when have you experienced a loss at a time when you least expected it?

2   How does it make you feel knowing that death and loss can come at any time? Where do you find hope in the midst of loss?

3   When have you experienced a bittersweet Christmas season? What happened? Who and what brought you comfort? Where did you find moments of joy during the season?

4   What scripture passages console you when you think about loved ones who have died? Why are these passages comforting to you?

5   Who in your life is grieving this Christmas season? How might you comfort them? If you are grieving this Christmas, what encouragement and support do you need from God and from others?

24 December

1   Do you enjoy attending Christmas Eve services at your church? Why or why not? How does celebrating Christ's birth with others differ from celebrating Christ on your own?

2   Have you ever felt too tired and unmotivated to attend a worship service? What did you do? Do you feel it is important to push yourself to go to church even when you don't feel like it? Why or why not?

3   Do you ever help set up for worship services or clean up afterward? Why or why not? How does helping in this way change your feelings about attending worship?

4   Recall a Christmas worship service that particularly lifted your spirits. What made that service special?

5   What scripture passages, prayers and hymns help you experience the joy of Christ's birth, even when responsibilities abound?

31 December

1 When has someone helped you unexpectedly in a time when you felt worried and overwhelmed? Why do you think they helped you? How did their assistance impact you?

2 How do your neighbours care for you? How do you care for your neighbours? Why is it so important to care for one another?

3 When someone shows you care and support, how do you thank them? Do you offer them something in return? Do you pray for them? Why or why not?

4 When has trouble brought you an unforeseen blessing? What happened? How did this blessing make a difference for you?

5 Who in your community needs your help today? What can you do for them?

Journal page

Become a Friend of BRF Ministries
and give regularly to support our ministry

We help people of all ages to grow in faith

We encourage and support individual Christians and churches as they serve and resource the changing spiritual needs of communities today.

Through **Anna Chaplaincy**
we're enabling churches to provide
spiritual care to older people

Through **Living Faith**
we're nurturing faith and resourcing
lifelong discipleship

Through **Messy Church**
we're helping churches to reach out
to families

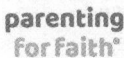

Through **Parenting for Faith**
we're supporting parents as they raise
their children in the Christian faith

Our ministry is only possible because of the generous support of individuals, churches, trusts and gifts in wills.

As we look to the future and make plans, **regular donations make a huge difference** in ensuring we can both start and finish projects well.

By becoming a Friend and giving regularly to our ministry, you are partnering with us in the gospel and helping change lives.

How your gift makes a difference

£2 a month — Helps us to give away **Living Faith** resources via food banks and chaplaincy services

£10 a month — Helps us to support parents and churches running the **Parenting for Faith** course

£5 a month — Helps us to support **Messy Church** volunteers and grow the wider network

£20 a month — Helps us to develop the reach of **Anna Chaplaincy** and improve spiritual care for older people

How to become a Friend of BRF Ministries

Online – set up a Direct Debit donation at **brf.org.uk/donate** or find out how to set up a Standing Order at **brf.org.uk/friends**

By post – complete and return the form opposite to 'Freepost BRF' (*no other address or stamp is needed*)

If you have any questions, or if you want to change your regular donation or stop giving in the future, do get in touch.

Contact the fundraising team

Email: **giving@brf.org.uk**
Tel: +44 (0)1235 462305
Post: Fundraising team, BRF Ministries, 15 The Chambers, Vineyard, Abingdon OX14 3FE

Registered with

FUNDRAISING **REGULATOR**

SHARING OUR VISION – MAKING A GIFT

I would like to make a donation to support BRF Ministries.
Please use my gift for:

☐ Where it is most needed ☐ Anna Chaplaincy ☐ Living Faith
☐ Messy Church ☐ Parenting for Faith

Title	First name/initials	Surname	
Address			
			Postcode
Email			
Telephone			
Signature			Date

Please accept my gift of:

☐ £2 ☐ £5 ☐ £10 ☐ £20 Other £ [   ]

by (*delete as appropriate*):

☐ Cheque/Charity Voucher payable to 'BRF'

☐ MasterCard/Visa/Debit card/Charity card

Name on card

Card no. ☐☐☐☐ ☐☐☐☐ ☐☐☐☐ ☐☐☐☐

Expires end ☐☐ M M ☐☐ Y Y Security code* ☐☐☐ *Last 3 digits on the reverse of the card

Signature	Date

Please complete other side of this form ➲

BRF Ministries Gift Aid Declaration
In order to Gift Aid your donation, you must tick the box below.

☐ I want to Gift Aid my donation and any donation I make in the future or have made in the past four years to BRF Ministries

I am a UK taxpayer and understand that if I pay less Income Tax and/or Capital Gains Tax in the current tax year than the amount of Gift Aid claimed on all my donations, it is my responsibility to pay any difference.

Please notify BRF Ministries if you want to cancel this Gift Aid declaration, change your name or home address, or no longer pay sufficient tax on your income and/or capital gains.

You can also give online at **brf.org.uk/donate**, which reduces our administration costs, making your donation go further.

Our ministry is only possible because of the generous support of individuals, churches, trusts and gifts in wills.

☐ I would like to leave a gift to BRF Ministries in my will.
    Please send me further information.

☐ I would like to find out about giving a regular gift to BRF Ministries.

For help or advice regarding making a gift, please contact our fundraising team +44 (0)1235 462305

Your privacy

We will use your personal data to process this transaction. From time to time we may send you information about the work of BRF Ministries that we think may be of interest to you. Our privacy policy is available at **brf.org.uk/privacy**. Please contact us if you wish to discuss your mailing preferences.

Registered with

FR

FUNDRAISING **REGULATOR**

➤ Please complete other side of this form

Please return this form to 'Freepost BRF'
No other address information or stamp is needed

BRF

Bible Reading Fellowship is a charity (233280) and company limited by guarantee (301324), registered in England and Wales

UR0325

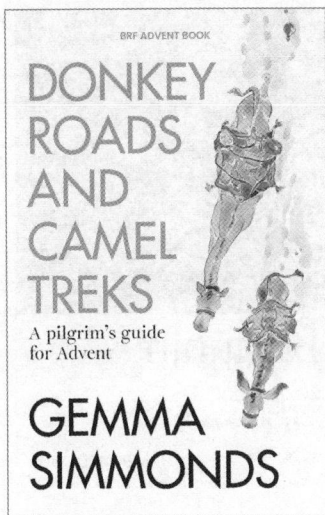

BRF ADVENT BOOK

DONKEY ROADS AND CAMEL TREKS

A pilgrim's guide for Advent

GEMMA SIMMONDS

The lectionary readings for Advent speak of making a straight path towards God, but many of us find our own route decidedly winding. Biblical characters in the story of the incarnation are called to set out on the road to discipleship using any means of carriage they can. This book offers user-friendly encouragement (with the occasional spur onwards) to explore what helps and what hinders us in this journey to deeper encounter with the flesh and blood God whom we find in scripture, in our lived experience and in the least of his sisters and brothers.

Donkey Roads and Camel Treks
A pilgrim's guide for Advent
Gemma Simmonds
978 1 80039 347 9   £9.99
brfonline.org.uk

Beginnings
and Endings
(and what happens in between)

Maggi Dawn
Daily Bible readings from Advent to Epiphany

Our everyday lives are full of small-scale beginnings and endings –
births, death, marriages, careers, house moves and so on. How do
the grand-scale beginnings and endings of Advent help to guide us
as we seek to follow Jesus in the 21st century? This new edition of a
classic Advent book reflects on the stories of six groups of people and
individual characters from the Bible. Each provides a focus on the idea
of beginnings and endings, and each gives us a glimpse into the human
experience in between.

Beginnings and Endings (and what happens in between)
Daily Bible readings from Advent to Epiphany
Maggi Dawn
978 1 80039 510 7 £9.99
brfonline.org.uk

How to encourage Bible reading in your church

BRF Ministries has been helping individuals connect with the Bible for over 100 years. We want to support churches as they seek to encourage church members into regular Bible reading.

Order a Bible reading resources pack
This pack is designed to give your church the tools to publicise our Bible reading notes. It includes:

- Sample Bible reading notes for your congregation to try.
- Publicity resources, including a poster.
- A church magazine feature about Bible reading notes.

The pack is free, but we welcome a £5 donation to cover the cost of postage. If you require a pack to be sent outside the UK or require a specific number of sample Bible reading notes, please contact us for postage costs. For more information about what the current pack contains, go to **brfonline.org.uk/pages/bible-reading-resources-pack**.

How to order and find out more
- Email **enquiries@brf.org.uk**
- Phone us on +44 (0)1865 319700 Mon–Fri 9.30–17.00.
- Write to us at BRF Ministries, 15 The Chambers, Vineyard, Abingdon OX14 3FE.

Keep informed about our latest initiatives
We are continuing to develop resources to help churches encourage people into regular Bible reading, wherever they are on their journey. Join our email list at **brfonline.org.uk/signup** to stay informed about the latest initiatives that your church could benefit from.

Subscriptions

The Upper Room is published in January, May and September.

Individual subscriptions
The subscription rate for orders for 4 or fewer copies includes postage and packing:

The Upper Room annual individual subscription   £21.30

Group subscriptions
Orders for 5 copies or more, sent to ONE address, are post free:
The Upper Room annual group subscription   £15.75

Please do not send payment with order for a group subscription. We will send an invoice with your first order.

Please note that the annual billing period for group subscriptions runs from 1 May to 30 April.

Copies of the notes may also be obtained from Christian bookshops.

Single copies of *The Upper Room* cost £5.25.

Prices valid until 30 April 2026.

Giant print version
The Upper Room is available in giant print for the visually impaired, from:

Torch Trust for the Blind
Torch House
Torch Way
Northampton Road
Market Harborough   Tel: +44 (0)1858 438260
LE16 9HL   **torchtrust.org**

All our Bible reading notes can be ordered online by visiting
brfonline.org.uk/subscriptions

☐ I would like to take out a subscription myself (complete your name and address details once)

☐ I would like to give a gift subscription (please provide both names and addresses)

Title .... First name/initials .... Surname ....

Address ....

.... Postcode ....

Telephone .... Email ....

Gift subscription name ....

Gift subscription address ....

.... Postcode ....

Gift message (20 words max. or include your own gift card):

....

....

Please send *The Upper Room* beginning with the January 2026 / May 2026 / September 2026 issue (*delete as appropriate*):

Annual individual subscription ☐ £21.30

Optional donation* to support the work of BRF Ministries £ ....

Total enclosed £ .... (cheques should be made payable to 'BRF')

*Please complete and return the Gift Aid declaration on page 159 to make your donation even more valuable to us.

Method of payment

Please charge my MasterCard / Visa with £ ....

Card no. ☐☐☐☐ ☐☐☐☐ ☐☐☐☐ ☐☐☐☐

Expires end ☐☐ ☐☐ Security code ☐☐☐ Last 3 digits on the reverse of the card

All our Bible reading notes can be ordered online by visiting brfonline.org.uk/subscriptions

☐ Please send me .... copies of *The Upper Room* January 2026 / May 2026 / September 2026 issue (*delete as appropriate*)

Title .... First name/initials .... Surname ....

Address ....

.... Postcode ....

Telephone .... Email ....

Please do not send payment with this order. We will send an invoice with your first order.

Christian bookshops: All good Christian bookshops stock our resources. For your nearest stockist, please contact us.

Telephone: The BRF office is open Mon–Fri 9.30–17.00. To place your order, telephone +44 (0)1865 319700.

Online: brfonline.org.uk/group-subscriptions

☐ Please send me a Bible reading resources pack to encourage Bible reading in my church

Please return this form with the appropriate payment to:
BRF Ministries, 15 The Chambers, Vineyard, Abingdon OX14 3FE

For terms and cancellation information, please visit **brfonline.org.uk/terms**.

Bible Reading Fellowship is a charity (233280) and company limited by guarantee (301324), registered in England and Wales

UR0325

To order

Online: brfonline.org.uk
Telephone: +44 (0)1865 319700 Mon–Fri 9.30–17.00

Delivery times within the UK are normally 15 working days. Prices are correct at the time of going to press but may change without prior notice.

BRF

Title	Price	Qty	Total
Donkey Roads and Camel Treks (BRF Advent book)	£9.99		
Beginnings and Endings (and what happens in between)	£9.99		

POSTAGE AND PACKING CHARGES			
Order value	UK	Europe	Rest of world
Under £7.00	£2.00		
£7.00–£29.99	£3.00	Available on request	Available on request
£30.00 and over	FREE		

Total value of books	
Postage and packing	
Donation*	
Total for this order	

* Please complete the Gift Aid declaration below

Please complete in BLOCK CAPITALS

Title .... First name/initials .... Surname ....

Address ....

.... Postcode ....

Acc. No. .... Telephone ....

Email ....

Gift Aid Declaration

giftaid it

Please treat as Gift Aid donations all qualifying gifts of money made (*tick all that apply*)

☐ today, ☐ in the past four years, ☐ and in the future **or** ☐ My donation does not qualify for Gift Aid.

I am a UK taxpayer and understand that if I pay less Income Tax and/or Capital Gains Tax in the current tax year than the amount of Gift Aid claimed on all my donations, it is my responsibility to pay any difference.

Please notify BRF Ministries if you want to cancel this declaration, change your name or home address, or no longer pay sufficient tax on your income and/or capital gains.

Method of payment

☐ Cheque (made payable to BRF) ☐ MasterCard / Visa

Card no. ☐☐☐☐ ☐☐☐☐ ☐☐☐☐ ☐☐☐☐

Expires end ☐☐ ☐☐ Security code ☐☐☐ Last 3 digits on the reverse of the card

Please return this form to:

BRF Ministries, 15 The Chambers, Vineyard, Abingdon OX14 3FE | **enquiries@brf.org.uk**
For terms and cancellation information, please visit brfonline.org.uk/terms.

Bible Reading Fellowship (BRF) is a charity (233280) and company limited by guarantee (301324), registered in England and Wales

![BRF Ministries logo] **BRF** Ministries

Inspiring people of all ages to grow in Christian faith

BRF Ministries is the
home of Anna Chaplaincy,
Living Faith, Messy Church
and Parenting for Faith

As a charity, our work would not be possible without
fundraising and gifts in wills.
To find out more and to donate,
visit brf.org.uk/give or call +44 (0)1235 462305